Robert E. Lee wrote:

—On the coming of the Civil War:

"I fear it is now out of the power of man and in God alone must be our trust. No act could give me so much pleasure as to restore peace to my country. God is our refuge and our strength. Let us humble ourselves before Him. Let us confess our sins and beseech Him to give a higher courage, a purer patriotism and a more determined will; that He will convert the hearts of our enemies; that He will hasten the time when war, with its sorrows and sufferings shall cease, and that He will give us a name and place among the nations of the earth."

—On the Bible:

"There are things in the old Book which I may not be able to explain, but I fully accept it as the infallible word of God and receive its teaching as inspired by the Holy Spirit."

—On his faith in God:

"I believe a kind God has ordered all things for our good.

My reliance is in the help of God.

At present I am not concerned with results. God's will ought to be our aim, and I am contented that His designs should be accomplished and not mine.

We must suffer patiently to the end, when all things will be made right.

I can only say that I am nothing but a poor sinner, trusting in Christ alone for salvation."

Robert E. Lee was one of the most truly remarkable men in our nation's history. The author writes, "I searched diligently for a flaw in Lee's character. There was none." What was this general's secret? He was a Christ-bearer. His secret was that he found the source of his strength and commitment in Christ.

ABOUT THE AUTHOR

Lee Roddy's journalism career began as a radio drama script writer. He has been a newspaper editor and columnist and writer for films and television.

Mr. Roddy is a former newspaper and radio broadcast executive with experience in advertising agencies and public relations. His award-winning newspaper was sold in 1973, and he is presently a full-time Christian writer. On the West Coast he writes and edits for prominent Christian leaders.

He has taught many writing courses including sessions at Mount Herman Christian Writers Conference and Biola College.

He is the author of numerous books and his published items number in the thousands both for secular and Christian publications. As a lifelong history buff he has written hundreds of newspaper columns on the subject. For several years he wrote and narrated the radio series "Your American Heritage."

Mr. Roddy is a graduate of Los Angeles State College and lives in California with his wife near Disneyland. He has two grown children.

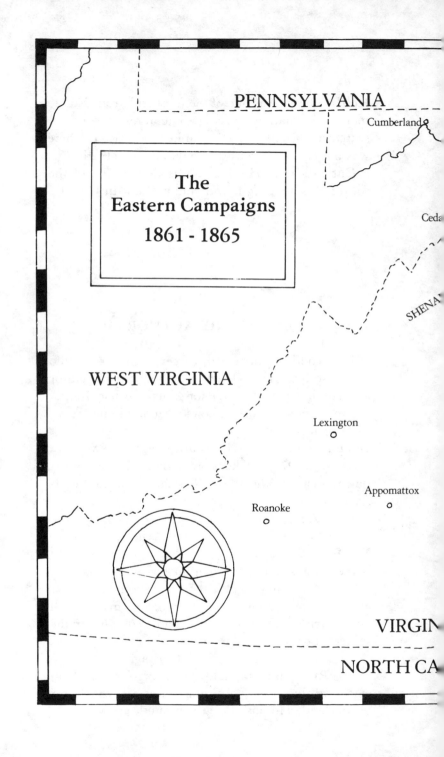

PENNSYLVANIA

Cumberland

The
Eastern Campaigns
1861 - 1865

Ced

SHENA

WEST VIRGINIA

Lexington
o

Appomattox
o

Roanoke
o

VIRGIN

NORTH CA

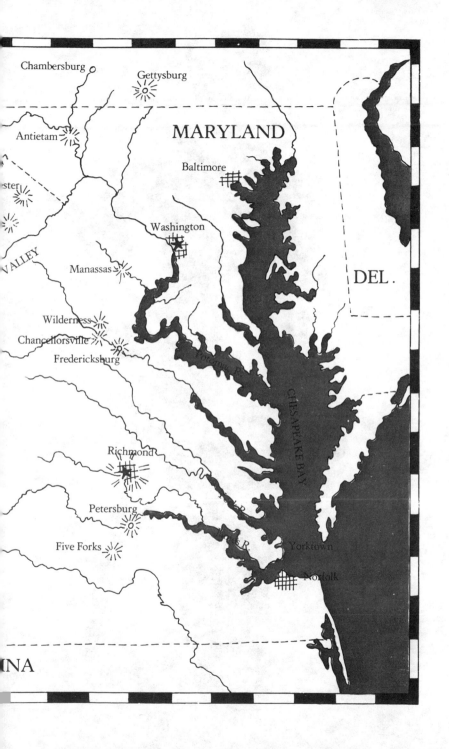

GALLANT CHRISTIAN SOLDIER
ROBERT E. LEE

by

LEE RODDY

Illustrated by **A. G. SMITH**

MOTT MEDIA

Milford, Michigan 48042

To my mother and father
Mr. and Mrs. T. L. (Jack) Roddy
For their fifty-fifth wedding anniversary

Norma Cournow Camp, Editor

LIBRARY OF CONGRESS CATALOGING IN PUBLICATION DATA

Roddy, Lee, 1921-
    Robert E. Lee, Christian general and gentleman.

    (The Sowers)
    Bibliography: p. 165
    Includes Index.

    SUMMARY: A biography of the leader of the Confederate forces during
the Civil War.
    1. Lee, Robert Edward, 1807-1870—Juvenile literature. 2. Generals—
Confederate States of America—Biography—Juvenile literature. 3. Con-
federate States of America. Army—Biography—Juvenile literature. [1. Lee,
Robert Edward, 1807-1870. 2. Generals] I. Smith, Albert Gray, 1945-
II. Title.

E467.1.L4R63   973.7'3'0924 [B]   77-7520
ISBN 0-915134-40-3 Paperback
ISBN 0-915134-97-7 Hardback

CONTENTS

FOREWORD

Writing about Robert E. Lee has given me an insight into one of the most truly remarkable men in our nation's history. As a former newspaper editor and writer of countless short historical biographies, I searched diligently for a flaw in Lee's character. I found none. I cannot say that of any other person I've read about or researched. I kept asking myself, "Why? What was his secret?" That led to this book.

Biography writing, by its very nature, requires that the writer depend upon the work of those who have gone before. Without these beacons to guide the way, no new work could be completed.

Therefore, I am deeply grateful to those men and women, living and dead, who helped provide factual material for this book, which takes a new slant on the subject, Lee.

It is impossible to pay all such people the full acknowledgment to which they are entitled, but I trust these few words will show my appreciation.

I am particularly indebted to Roy P. Basler, Chief, The Library of Congress, for permission to consult the national manuscript collection and Lee Family material. I also thank John C. Broderick for permission through heirs to consult the DeButts-Ely Collection of Robert E. Lee family material. I am also grateful to John W. Dudley, Head, Archives Branch, Virginia State Library, for suggesting Richard Harwell's one-volume abridgement of Douglas Southall Freeman's *R. E. Lee*. Freeman had consulted all primary source material in libraries of that area. I also relied heavily on the extensive materials and rare books made available to me by Virginia J. Renner, Registrar, The Huntington Library, San Marino, California. Some of the other works I consulted are listed elsewhere in this book; I thank the various permissions departments for permission to quote portions of their books.

Since personal recollections of Lee as a boy are limited, I used some imaginative fiction there. But wherever a fact was known, I included it to give Lee's boyhood every bit of historic accuracy possible.

Lee's adult life, from teenager on, is well documented. Names, major events and places are real. I tried to tell the story as those who lived it remembered and recorded it. I avoided romanticizing his adult life except in a few instances where minor incidents were needed to flesh out the narrative before he became famous. In each case, I tried to be as accurate as possible, based on known circumstances. If there are points on which accuracy fails, it is due to my mind and not to my heart.

I wish to express my thanks, too, to my wife, Cicely, who let me spend so much time with Lee during the research and writing of this book. My son, Steve, and daughter, Susan, were also very helpful in encouraging me to keep on with the book when the going got rough, as it did from time to time. Mrs. Norma Camp was especially helpful in editing and criticizing the manuscript from her vantage of having been born in Petersburg and having her home in Richmond. She provided valuable details which no other resource offered me.

It is my fervent prayer that young readers will be inspired by this truly remarkable man, Lee, who lived his faith as few of us succeed in doing. I confess that I agree with one biographer who wrote, if Protestants had saints, Lee would be one. If this book will help readers find for themselves the secret of Robert E. Lee, and claim the same Christ-bearers' source for themselves, the story I have told is well worth the effort it took to tell it.

Lee Roddy
Costa Mesa, California

Chapter 1

Plantations and Poverty

The cry of a newborn baby drifted faintly from the plantation house known as Stratford Hall. A young slave outside the great house rubbed her hands against the cold. She cocked her head slightly, straining to hear. The sharp January wind made hearing impossible.

A slave with her hair tied up in a red cloth opened the door a crack. "It's a boy!"

The young slave threw up her arms in joy. "A boy! Ol' Marse Lee got hisself another son!"

The house slave opened the heavy door a little wider. She motioned for the other woman to come closer.

"Poor Mrs. Lee! She didn't want that child!" Jessy said. Her red headcloth bounced up and down.

"How you know that?"

"I know, that's how," Jessy said. "She already got three mouths to feed, and her husband is trying to stay out of debtor's prison!" Jessy's headcloth bobbed rapidly.

The young woman raised a warning finger.
"Don't you go talking that way! Marse Light Horse
Harry Lee is a mighty fine gentleman! He was a
Revolutionary War general that fought with
Washington. Three times Marse Lee been
governor of Virginy!"

"Makes no difference now," Jessy sniffed. "He
lent a plenty money to Mr. Morris, and he didn't
pay it back. Then Mr. Lee spent money for land,
and he lost that, too. Fact of the matter is, he's
already lost everything he owned except this old
mansion. And he'd lose that if it was his'n, but the
creditors can't take it. The house belonged to the
first Mrs. Lee, and she left it to their first born son,
Henry."

The young slave nodded slowly. "You right
about that, honey. Young Henry will inherit this
whole place soon, from what I hear tell." She
turned, "I'll go spread the news it's a boy."

Jessy closed the immense door. The slave
glanced down the cold hallway, thinking about
the fireplaces. All except one wing of the mansion
was boarded up because there wasn't enough
wood to keep the hearths warm.

A quick sound of feet snapped her dark eyes up.
A gray-haired slave hurried past, making little
moaning sounds deep in her heavy throat.

"What's the matter?" Jessy whispered, her hand
on the headcloth.

"She's dead!"

"Who's dead?" Jessy asked.

"Who you think?" she called over her broad
shoulders. "Mrs. Lee, that's who!"

The younger slave swayed against the cold
walls. "Poor Mr. Lee! Widower again!" She began
to rock in grief. "Poor Mrs. Lee! I should have
knowed it! Catching that heavy cold in December, riding in that old open carriage!"

The older slave hurried back, moving her heavy body with surprising ease. "Don't you stand around a'moaning and a'groaning. Take this to the midwife, and be quick about it, you hear."

Jessy took the clean cloths and moved fearfully toward the birth chamber. She fought back tears as she peered cautiously toward the heavy dark bed with the white canopy.

"Where's Ruth?" the midwife snapped. "Why you standing there staring? Get Ruth back in here!"

Jessy retreated uncertainly to where she could hail the heavy woman. "You better git back in there!"

The gray-haired slave heaved her bulk forward. "Why? What's the matter?"

"Her eyes!"

"What about them?"

"They're open!" Jessy said.

"Well, she's dead, just the same." The older woman puffed past. "You don't know nothing about birthing and dying!"

"I saw her move," Jessy said weakly. But the older slave had not heard. The dark door closed slowly behind her.

That cold January 19, 1807, Robert Edward Lee had entered a family full of trouble. But there was pleasant news which soon swept through the slave quarters. His mother was not dead. She had simply lapsed into a coma after the birth of her dark-eyed, black-haired son. When she awoke, she named him after her two brothers.

Slowly, Mrs. Lee regained her health while her well-known husband vainly tried to pay off his creditors. It was hard on Light Horse Harry Lee whose family were rich Virginia landowners. The Lees of Virginia were famous and honored back to their family in England. But that made no

difference to the men who demanded that Henry
Lee pay them the money owed. The fact that Mrs.
Lee was the heir of Virginia wealth also made no
difference to the creditors. They wanted money
now!

Mrs. Lee tried not to think of what was going to
happen if her husband couldn't find some way to
satisfy his clamoring creditors. As she carried the
baby about the great old mansion she thought
about what Stratford Hall had once been.

It had been built as a fortress in the 1720's by a
descendant of the first Lee to come from England.
It sat well back from the Potomac, perhaps a mile.
A view had been cut through the trees so the river
could be seen from the great house.

In the way of mothers, Mrs. Lee patted her new
son. She glanced around the once-stately mansion.
"Our poor dwelling!" she sighed.

In a few months, Robert was toddling around
the large, sunny room with the big canopied bed
where he had been born. The room had very high
ceilings and tall windows. Next to the
bedchamber was his nursery.

Long before Robert was old enough to
understand, his older brother, Sydney Smith Lee,
age five, showed him a cannon ball. It was nearly
covered with grass outside the kitchen.

With all the excitement of having something
important to share, Smith said, "Look, Robert! A
British man-o-war fired it from the river during
the Rev-a—Revolution."

Smith had a little trouble pronouncing the war
in which their father had become famous, but
Robert didn't mind. He listened as Smith pointed,
"The ship sailed right up the Potomac there and
turned the big guns on our house."

Robert shaded his dark eyes with a small hand

to see the water. This was an early introduction to war for Robert.

Another brother, Charles Carter Lee, nine years older than Robert, told him the twin chimneys of their house had been used long ago by men for hiding places when defending Stratford Hall against Indians and other attackers.

Robert's seven-year-old sister, Anne Kinlock Lee, delighted in babying her little brother. Robert's tongue pronounced his sister's name as Wanzi. And it stuck as her special name.

Wanzi's young ears had already picked up enough plantation gossip to know the Lees of Virginia were wealthy. There were many Lees, and nearly all were Virginia's high society. There were lawyers, politicians and naval officers in the Lee cousins and uncles. But their branch of the family was now poor.

Wanzi took Robert's small hand and helped him up their steep front stairs. One of the few remaining male slaves held the big front door open for the master's son and daughter. The slave showed a missing tooth as he grinned.

Robert smiled back, his dark eyes flashing their gentle nature. The boy struck the heavy chains on the mansion door. He smiled at his sister and the slave, pleased with the rattling sound. The slave's face grew sober.

Wanzi lowered her eyes. She was quite young, but she understood there was something disgraceful about having to chain the mansion door to keep out the creditors.

As Robert grew, his love for exploring the stables grew also.

"Up you go!" said Mr. Lee, boosting young Robert to the back of a gentle mare. "Now, just sit quietly until you get the feel of it. I'll lead the horse."

A male slave grinned approvingly at the boy sitting calmly on the mare's back. "Young Marse Robert sits right nice. He'll ride good someday. Yes, sir!"

The fifty-one-year-old father nodded. "If he wasn't such a little toddler, I'd say he already has shown an eye for good horseflesh. Did you notice how he wanted to ride this one?"

From the first, Robert liked horses. His father taught him from the earliest possible age to appreciate good horses. This was natural for Light Horse Harry Lee with his experience as major general of cavalry under George Washington.

Mr. Lee also taught Robert the values of moral courage and personal integrity. These were about all the creditors had not taken from Henry Lee.

In 1809, when Robert was two years old, the creditors won. Gray-haired Henry Lee was thrown into Westmoreland County Jail because he could not meet his creditors' demands.

Young Robert didn't understand, of course. He only knew his mother looked sad much of the time. All the long time that her husband was away, Mrs. Lee said nothing of his absence except things would be better "after his release from his present situation."

She didn't say Robert's father was in jail, and the little boy wouldn't have understood. Robert missed his father—their walks to the smokehouse and around the formal garden, small stable and coachhouse. He missed his father's strong hands lifting him onto a horse.

But in the father's absence, Robert grew close to his mother.

"Would you look at that?" chuckled the heavy slave who had been in the bedchamber at Robert's birth. "For a woman who didn't want that child, she sure is mighty fond of him."

"Can't blame her none," the male slave with the missing tooth observed. "Fine looking boy, he is. Quiet, sober-like for such a little one. And he sure do love his mother."

Ann Carter Lee, second wife of Lee, had been one of the richest heiresses in Virginia when she married the dashing ex-cavalry general. Her father had not approved of the widower who had come wooing Ann. Mr. Carter, owner of thousands of acres and hundreds of slaves at the mansion called Shirley, had thought his daughter could marry better.

When Henry was thrown into debtor's prison, it appeared his father-in-law was right. Yesterday's cavalry glories meant nothing.

Mrs. Lee spent part of the time her husband was away in teaching her youngest son her own strong Christian faith. Bible in hand, she took the boy upon her lap to teach him about the goodness and wisdom of God. Then, easing off her lap, he knelt beside her to whisper his first prayers.

While Henry Lee was in jail, his family waited uncertainly at Stratford Hall. Time was running out there for Mrs. Lee, her three sons and daughter. Her stepson had come of age. Henry could now claim the mansion willed him by his late mother.

Young Henry soon told his stepmother and her family they could stay as guests in the great home which he now owned.

But Mr. Lee refused the offer in the spring of 1810 when he was released from prison.

"You'll like Alexandria," Henry Lee assured his wife for perhaps the tenth time. "Many of your friends are there. A rented house won't be so bad. You'll see."

Mrs. Lee's eyes showed their tiredness, but she

smiled at her husband. "I'll be happy, dear. So will the children; all four of them."

"Soon be five," he mused.

"It'll be all right, dear. Now, let me get the packing supervised in Robert's nursery." Ann Carter Lee kissed her husband lightly on the cheek and moved off through the big mansion. Four-year-old Robert followed her.

For a long moment, his father gazed thoughtfully after dark-haired Robert. He was keenly aware of the growing attachment between mother and son.

"Well," Henry Lee mused to himself, "she's certainly had enough problems. It's good for her to have someone so close to her."

The master's pensive mood was caught by a young woman slave. "Poor ol' Marse Lee! No money to tutor his young'uns. Having to live in his son's house! No wonder they's moving."

The heavy woman slave warned, "Don't you go talking like that! The Lees is quality; it'll turn out fine for them in Alexandria. You'll see."

"I wonder! You see what Marse Robert's got to take with him? A pony, a cart and one family dog! That sure ain't much."

Light Horse Harry Lee went to his wife. "I'll take Robert for a last look around," he said. He reached a strong hand out to his small son.

Slowly they strolled past the great mansion and red sandy fields. They came to the smokehouse. Robert sniffed the pleasant fragrance of wood smoke which drifted from the small building. His father laughed. "You like that, do you, son? Well, so do I! Nothing smells much better than a smokehouse . . ."

"Kitchen," Robert said, pointing.

His father laughed again. "You're right, Robert! The kitchen does smell better. Come on; let's go

see if we can find some cornbread and fresh
butter."

The family moved to a small brick house on
Cameron Street in Alexandria. Less than eight
thousand people lived there when Robert arrived
with his parents, sister and two brothers.

One of the first things the family did was to
attend the Episcopalian Christ Church. "That's
where General Washington worshipped," Light
Horse Harry Lee said quietly. "That's where our
family will worship too."

Months slipped away and the general was
restless. Twice he had been to prison for debt.
During his second imprisonment in Spotsylvania
prison he wrote a book about his experiences in
the Revolution. He hoped the revenue from the
book sales would help pay his debts.

Another ray of hope glimmered for Light Horse
Harry Lee when his son, Robert, was five years
old. The War of 1812 with England meant soldiers
would again be needed. Although he was in poor
health, the fifty-six-year-old, experienced general
sought to again put on his country's uniform.

"It'll be just as it was thirty years ago," he told his
wife. "They'll need me, and I'll go. But there won't
be General Washington to lead this time."

Mrs. Lee patted Robert on the back. "You run
out and play," she said. She fondly watched the
boy as he bounced happily out of the room. Then
Mrs. Lee looked lovingly at her husband. "You're a
little older now, dear," she said gently. "They may
not—"

"They'll want me! I'm not too old! But if they
don't send my orders through soon, I'll just cross
the river and hurry them along!"

"But I could use you more at home, Henry!
Since Catherine Mildred was born, and Robert's
still so young—"

Her husband waved an impatient hand. "If I
don't get my orders by tomorrow, I'm going to
Washington City."

The next morning Robert waved good-bye to
his father as he left to find out why he had not been
recalled to duty. It was a warm, humid July day
when the aging soldier rode away. Robert
watched him with thoughtful eyes.

Mrs. Lee took her son's hand. "Come, Robert.
Let's pray."

A few days later, people began hurrying to the
rented Lee house in Alexandria.

"What's the matter?" Robert asked his mother.
"Where's Father?"

Mrs. Lee knelt beside her son. She was still weak
from the birth of her daughter although months
had passed. Many things were taking a toll of Mrs.
Lee's strength.

"There was a riot," she said. "Angry men tried to
destroy a newspaper office. Your father aided the
owner and was hurt, Robert."

One man had died and eleven had been badly
injured in the riot. Hot candle wax had been
dropped onto Light Horse Harry Lee's
unconscious form to see if he was still alive. One
drunken rioter cut off the general's nose tip with a
penknife.

Little Robert E. Lee didn't know these details,
but he knew something terrible had happened
when important men began arriving at his home.
Among them was President James Madison.

The president spoke to the boy about
"barbarians and hypocrites" who had seriously
wounded Light Horse Harry Lee. Robert listened
gravely as President Madison said, "Let your
father's honor and matchless gallantry set an
example that you will never forget."

Soon there was more excitement. The British

burned the nation's capitol across the river. Robert could see the smoke from Alexandria. Everyone was very excited, for Washington was in flames.

Weeks later Mrs. Lee finished teaching Robert his lessons. He knelt at her knee and prayed as she had taught him. When he stood, his mother put her arms around his neck.

"Your father is going to take a trip," she explained. "Maybe he'll feel better down in the warm Caribbean Islands. Will you help me like a big boy while Father's away?"

Robert and his mother grew closer than before when Henry Lee left on a cruise to regain his health. Mrs. Lee had other children, but Robert was especially close to her.

Mrs. Lee tutored Robert until he was old enough to attend school. She was deeply religious, and taught her son to share her strong faith in God. The difficulties which she endured were not punishments from an angry Lord, as some whispered. Mrs. Lee knew that the Lord gave His children tests to help them grow strong. It was for their own good that the Lee family experienced their many problems.

When Robert showed his strong will in his father's absence, an aunt offered suggestions to Mrs. Lee. "Whip and pray," she said, "and pray and whip."

One evening Robert sat thinking about his father. He missed him greatly. "Mother, tell me stories about Father again," he begged.

Mrs. Lee told Robert that his father was a war hero who served under George Washington. "It was your father who wrote at General Washington's death: 'First in war, first in peace and first in the hearts of his countrymen,' " Robert's mother explained. "Your father won important battles for Washington during the Revolution."

The day came when Robert left home to begin his school years. The Carter family from which his mother was descended was big enough to have their own school. Eastern View became Robert's first classroom.

Robert was very close to his many wealthy cousins, both on the Lee and the Carter side. Although Robert's branch had suffered great financial losses, the dignity and honor of the Southern family was stronger than the loss of money.

When Robert finished school for the day, he hurried home to his mother. A visiting cousin, Edmond, watched Robert feed the pet rabbits and do the shopping.

Robert explained in his soft Southern tones, "Mother's developing such severe rheumatism she can't get around well any more."

Edmond nodded and offered a blade of grass to a twitching-nosed rabbit. Edmond didn't say anything to Robert about what he had heard: Ann Carter Lee was fast becoming an invalid.

Robert's mother taught him to keep house. He did the chores without complaining. But he was also all boy, and loved to roam through the hills and woods. He hunted ducks in King George's Meadow, a marshy area outside of town. Robert shot partridge in the woods and fished in the river.

"Sure, I know Robert," a neighbor boy told a visitor to town. "He's an expert oarsman and swimmer. He likes to swim in the Potomac, and nobody can beat him on horseback or afoot."

One day a slave drove in from the tobacco plantations with a wagonload of cured tobacco for the wharfs at Alexandria. He told the slaves who helped unload that he had seen Robert playing just outside town.

"Oh, could dat boy run! I see him run a foot race up a hill and beat other boys mounted on horses! He run two miles faster than anybody else!"

Robert entered his teens as a dark-eyed, dark-haired and very gentlemanly youth. He progressed to Alexandria Academy as his older brothers grew up and moved away.

Carter, the oldest, earned a law degree from Harvard. Smith entered the navy. Robert's older sister had an arm amputated in one of the continuing tragic events which seemed to plague Robert Lee's family. Catherine Mildred, born in 1811, was still at home when a shocking letter came from a friend.

Robert remembered another letter that his father had written in February 1818. Henry Lee was anxious to return home although he wasn't really well even after all the years of seeking better health in warmer climates. He had written he was coming home after finally finding passage on a ship bound for some Southern port "not yet decided."

Now Robert read the new letter which had come. " 'He was on his way to Savannah where he hoped to find a stage . . .' " a friend had written, " 'when an illness befell him, he asked to be placed ashore on Cumberland Island.' "

Robert stopped reading and glanced at his mother. She was dry-eyed, steeling herself for the words which would cut deep into her. "That's an island off Georgia, near the Florida border."

Mrs. Lee nodded and motioned for her son to continue reading. Robert cleared his throat. " 'Your husband had served with General Nathanael Green in the Revolution. This island is his home, or was, until he died, in 1786.' "

Mrs. Lee made an impatient sound. She was now so badly crippled with rheumatism that she could not hold things in her hands without difficulty. "Just read it rapidly to yourself, please Robert; then tell me what the letter says."

Robert nodded and quickly skimmed the letter. "General Green's daughter and her husband made Father welcome while he was a guest in their home, but he seldom did anything but walk in the garden with their small son. Two surgeons were sent by the army and navy, but it was too late by the time they learned Father was on the island."

Robert paused, looking carefully at his mother. "Father was buried with full military honors in the Green's own family cemetery. Maybe—Maybe we can go there sometime."

When he was sixteen, Robert finished his formal education. But 1823 was a bleak year for Robert's

future, for there was no money to go on to college.
He and his mother had only the barest necessities.

"There's one hope," he told his mother. "I've
been thinking about applying for entrance to the
U.S. Military Academy at West Point."

His mother was silent a long time, thinking. As
the son of a Revolutionary War hero and former
governor of Virginia, Robert was certainly eligible
for appointment as a cadet. Yes, he might just be
admitted.

Robert applied for entrance, and on March 11,
1824, at seventeen, was appointed to the military
academy by President James Monroe. It was the
beginning of an historic military career for Robert
E. Lee. That career was underlaid with a secret
that gave him a peace and calmness that people
noticed.

Chapter 2

West Point Soldier

Robert had to wait fifteen months before entering West Point. There were only about 6,000 men in the entire standing army, and forty officers graduated annually from the military academy.

The neighbors talked privately about the boy's devotion to his now invalided mother. "I never saw the like," an older woman said across a picket fence. "That boy carries his mother in his arms and puts her in the carriage for a ride nearly everyday."

"He's a wonder," a younger woman said, plucking dead leaves from a yellow rose bush. "He hurries home from school instead of going off with the other boys. He hitches up that old gentle mare and away they go, just as though she wasn't totally crippled and helpless!"

The older woman sighed. "Poor Mrs. Lee! What a troubled life she's had! And now, confined to that rolling chair."

"Wonder what she'll do when Robert goes away to West Point?" the younger woman mused.

"She'll be home with only her daughters." They watched the Lee carriage rumble past.

Robert touched the reins lightly to the mare. "Where would you like to go tonight, Mother?"

"It doesn't matter. It's such a lovely evening that any place will be fine."

"How about letting the mare have her head?"

Mrs. Lee laughed lightly. "Why not, indeed?"

The horse moved slowly past Christ Church with its square, two-story brick solidness.

"Remember when you were a little boy," Mrs. Lee asked above the horse's steady hoofbeats, "how you learned the catechism before you could read?"

"I'm glad you taught me the basics of our faith," her son replied.

The mare's steady clip-clop filled the quiet evening air. Mother and son rode in thoughtful silence through the streets of Alexandria.

The next afternoon Robert did the shopping for his mother. He called for his little sister, Mildred, to hold the door open. When she hastened to obey, he carried the large box of groceries from the buggy to the kitchen. He grinned at Mildred as he squeezed by her.

"You're right on time, as usual," she said, glancing at the clock. "Punctual Robert E. Lee!"

Mrs. Lee looked up from her rolling chair. "Mildred and I were just talking about you, Robert."

"Oh?" He began putting the flour away.

"Yes," Mildred said, peering into the box, "we wonder if you're going to get impatient waiting for the academy to have a seat for you."

"I've been thinking about attending that new school Benjamin Hallowell is opening."

"He's a neighbor," Mrs. Lee mused. "He is said to be a nice man; a Quaker, I hear."

Robert smiled at his Episcopalian mother. "I thought I would study mathematics under Mr. Hallowell. I believe you've already taught me my Christian principles."

Mildred remarked, "I thought you learned enough about mathematics from that Irishman, Mr. Leary."

"It was really just an introduction to the subject. I need to know as much as possible before West Point."

"I think Mother has taught you more than anybody, Robert," Mildred said.

Robert glanced lovingly at his mother. She had planted the seeds of faith in him. She had taught him to read the Bible and instilled in him the importance of prayer. But most important, she had taught him to trust in Christ as his Savior.

"Father taught me many things, too," Robert said. "I found one of his old letters a couple days ago. He wrote, 'you should learn to swim, ride, shoot, box, dance and use the sword . . .' "

" 'But only in self-defense,' " Mrs. Lee finished. "I remember that letter."

"Both of you taught me many things," Robert observed. "Nobody could ask for more."

In the tradition of Virginia and the South, young Robert had been taught to be a gentleman in all ways. This quality greatly influenced his life. He was deeply bred to the aristocratic way. But the money which went with such breeding had long since been lost from Mrs. Lee.

"I've taught you all I can," Mrs. Lee said. "Now perhaps it's Mr. Hallowell's turn to try you with higher mathematics."

The Quaker schoolteacher was impressed with his teen-age math student. "Robert E. Lee entered my school," Hallowell told a friend, "in the winter of 1824-25 to study mathematics, preparatory to his going to West Point.

"He was a most exemplary student in every respect. He was never behind in his studies, never failed in a single recitation, was perfectly observant of the rules and regulations and respectful in all his deportment to teachers and fellow students."

Hallowell added a keen insight into the character of his prize eighteen-year-old pupil: "His specialty was finishing up."

Robert's attention to detail was a source of pride to his teacher. Hallowell explained that Robert "imparted a neatness and finish to everything he undertook. One of the branches of mathematics he studied with me was conic sections, in which some of the diagrams were very complicated."

Hallowell added that Robert drew the diagrams on a slate although he knew the "drawing would have to be removed to make room for the next" yet he "drew each one with as much accuracy and finish . . . as if it were to be engraved and printed."

"The same traits he exhibited at my school, he carried with him to West Point," Hallowell said.

On October 14, 1824, the Lee family was to be honored with a visit from a famous Frenchman. Lafayette, who had fought alongside Light Horse Harry Lee in the Revolution, was coming.

When Mrs. Lee heard the dignified old warrior was to visit, she hastily called in her two daughters and son. Anne, whom Robert had called Wanzi, was unmarried at twenty-four years old. She suffered from a nervous disorder. Mildred, only thirteen, was very excited at her mother's news.

"Lafayette? Coming here? Oh, Mother! What'll we do? We'll have to clean the house, do special

cooking and figure on just everybody coming to
see Father's old comrade in arms."

Wanzi caught the spirit. "Imagine! The marquis
coming here, to this house, to pay his respects to
Father's family! Oh, I'm so glad it's a beautiful
time of year."

Robert's quiet dark eyes looked through the
window of their brick home. It belonged to one of
the numerous Lee relatives who had made the rent
reasonable.

"It is beautiful outdoors," Robert said. His
mother's and sisters' eyes followed his gaze. The
autumn display of colored leaves clung to the
trees.

"Well, don't just stand there!" Mildred cried.
"Let's get ready for our visitor."

Lafayette, like Henry Lee, had been a major
general in the American (then called Colonial)
Army. The Frenchman had been made a United
States officer by act of Congress. Now he had
returned to tour the United States.

The Oronoco Street house vibrated with
excitement as the Frenchman's carriage stopped
outside. He entered the room where Mrs. Lee was
waiting to receive him. She had dressed in her
finest black clothing and been made comfortable
in a high-backed chair.

The stately visitor greeted Mrs. Lee and her two
daughters. The alert old soldier's eyes settled on
Robert.

"How tall are you?" Lafayette asked.

"Five feet, eleven inches, sir," Robert said.

The general pursed his lips and partially closed
one eye. He looked at Robert's dark hair and deep
brown eyes. Lafayette mused to himself, Robert's
head is massive, and probably crammed with
brains. The youth's neck is powerful but in
proportion to his big chest.

Mrs. Lee, reading the old general's eyes, saw he was pleased with Robert. Her husband would have been proud to see the look in Lafayette's eyes. It was obvious he was impressed with his old comrade's youngest son.

When Lafayette had gone, the Lee household returned to normal. Robert continued his education with Benjamin Hallowell through the spring of 1825.

The hot, humid summer came on. It was nearly time for Robert's departure to West Point. He had to be there by June 30.

His mother had a hard time facing her son's going away.

"How can I ever live without him?" she exclaimed to a friend. "He has been son, daughter, protector; he has been all-in-all to me!"

June drew to a close. The time had come. Eighteen-year-old Robert E. Lee took steamer and stagecoach from Virginia to New York.

At the U.S. Military Academy on the west bank of the Hudson River a new life began for Robert E. Lee. West Point was only twenty-three years old when he stepped onto the dreary, wind-swept parade grounds. The old buildings were from the Revolution when West Point had been a river fort. There was nothing cheerful about the ugly structures.

Lee turned his eyes from the man-made dreariness to the beautiful Hudson River below the cliffs. Tree-covered mountains surrounded the military academy.

Lee was assigned to a tent on the windy parade and campground called the plain.

As the cadets lined up for the first time, a freckled-face boy next to Lee whispered, "I hear the food is poor, the discipline is strict and rules are impossible to keep without getting demerits."

Lee said nothing. He turned his attention to the staff sergeant who was standing stiffly before them.

"You will obey these instructions: Cadets are not allowed off the grounds. There will be no drinking or smoking."

A moan, half in fun, rippled through the 105 cadets. The freckled youth next to Lee made a face.

"There goes all my fun," the cadet whispered.

Lee said nothing. He did not smoke or drink, and he planned to continue that way. He had come to study the art of the soldier. His whole attention was given to that.

Lee studied hard and shared the barracks with other fourth classmen (freshmen).

The freckled-face cadet who had stood with Lee that first day was the first of the new cadets to be reprimanded. He was charged with using tobacco and playing cards. He came angrily into the barracks after seeing the superintendent.

"Colonel Sylvanus Thayer is a hard, hard man!" he said with great feeling. "He sat there with that little curl of hair over his forehead and not a trace of human kindness about him! He sounded like ice breaking on a pond when he spoke! And he wasn't a bit gentle about it, either."

The cadet finally settled down, muttering to himself about his demerits. Lee saw that the cadet soon tired of his books and sneaked a novel out of his bedding. This was also forbidden.

In a few days, the cadet was muttering again. He had another demerit for being off limits.

Lee did not raise his eyes from his book. He wondered how long the rebellious cadet would last.

In a short time, another demerit for having cooking utensils in his room caused the freckled-face youth to resign. He also faced court-martial and dismissal for having engaged in a bloody fistfight.

He was the first of Lee's class to drop out.

Lee started off slowly in a very hard school. His competition was a New Yorker, Charles Mason, a dark-haired cadet. An Ohio cadet named Catharinus Buckingham and a Georgian called William Hartford were also ahead of Lee in the beginning. Soon, however, Lee was gaining, moving up to third in mathematics. He was fifth in French by January 1826.

However, as Lee must have known, the Bible says ". . . that the race is not to the swift" (Ecclesiastes 9:11). Lee kept plugging along. At the end of another six months, he was third in general merit. Only Mason and Hartford were ahead of him. Lee was listed as a "distinguished cadet."

At the end of his first year, Cadet Lee was appointed staff sergeant. This unusual honor was not for grades alone, but because Lee had received no demerits in a very tough system.

The cadets who had entered West Point with Lee continued to drop out. Some of them could not stand the strict discipline and the hard studies. Many got into fights, drinking at a near-by tavern or were simply absent from parade and were dismissed.

By June 1827, Cadet Lee had earned a furlough with general merit ratings second only to Mason. With the course half finished, Lee was slowly pulling ahead of the other cadets.

After being away for two years without a furlough, Lee went home for two months. He took with him a nickname, "Marble Model." It was probably meant in fun, but there was seriousness in it, too.

His nephew, Fitzhugh Lee, proudly described Lee to his friends: "His clothes looked nice and new. His crossbelts, collar and summer trousers were white as the driven snow mounting guard upon the mountain top. And his brass breast and waist plates were mirrors to reflect the image of the inspectors."

Everyone was noticing how very handsome Robert E. Lee was that hot summer.

Among them was the blue-eyed daughter of rich George Washington Park Custis of Arlington. Mary Anne Randolph Custis was the only surviving child of the plantation owner whose mansion was truly immense. Mary was heiress to this fine home which stood on a ridge overlooking Washington across the Potomac River.

Lee and the heiress had known each other as children when they had met during visits to Mrs. Lee's family home at Shirley on the James River. There was speculation about Mary Custis and Cadet Lee.

"I don't think her father will take kindly to anybody as poor as Cadet Lee when there are other young men around with as much money as Mr. Custis."

"Nobody," another girl replied, "is as rich as George Washington Park Custis."

"I have to admit you're right. If you count Mr. Custis' thousands of acres and many slaves, well, that's rich enough."

Lee was welcome at the various social functions given by his relatives. He was known to tease the girls, but never unkindly.

The men of Virginia also liked Lee, who was one of them. He was bred to the aristocracy with its strict code of conduct for gentlemen.

Lee wore his gray cadet uniform with white bullet buttons to take his mother to visit a Carter cousin.

"She looks quite unwell," a sparkling young girl said as she watched Lee and his mother talking with the cousin. "I wonder if he has any thoughts about leaving her behind while he goes back to West Point?"

Her male companion looked at Cadet Lee with frankly admiring eyes. "Of course! Everybody knows how devoted he is to her. But he's a Virginian, and duty will take him back to the academy."

Lee finished his furlough and returned to West

Point. He renewed his efforts and the following
June was rewarded by ranking second in physics,
third in chemistry and third in drawing. Since he
had no demerits, he was given an even higher
honor: corps adjutant.

Lee finished his final year with the rating of top
student in artillery and tactics. He was second in
general merit behind Charles Mason, who later
resigned from the army and spent his life as a
civilian.

Robert E. Lee, West Point Class of '29, was
breveted a second lieutenant with the Corps of
Engineers, his chosen field. "Brevet" means he got
the rank but no extra pay.

At age twenty-two, Brevet Second Lieutenant
Robert E. Lee took his earned $103.58 in cash and
started home on a two-month furlough.

His orders called for him to report in August for
his first military assignment on Cockspur Island in
the Savannah River, Georgia.

Lee took a ship south from West Point to find his
mother was dying. That hot summer, Lee cared
for his mother with untiring devotion.

On July 26, 1829, Ann Hill Carter Lee died.
Robert stood by her bed as she slipped away, a
woman who had suffered physically and
emotionally most of her adult life.

Grief swelled in his throat. He sighed, realizing
his mother was with her Savior. But he would miss
her deeply.

She had left behind a priceless legacy for
Virginia and the nation in Robert E. Lee, newly
graduated from West Point.

Chapter 3

Lee Takes a Bride

Fort Pulaski on Cockspur Island was a good place for insects but no place for men in the summer of 1829. Lieutenant Lee's patient drawing skills were used to sketch the fortification built as part of a chain along the Atlantic seaboard.

The swampy island in the Savannah River gave the young West Point graduate his first practical engineering experience. He worked in the mud and water, shoring up the fort which sat like a fly on a turtle-shaped island.

Nothing escaped Lee's careful eye—not even the diamond-back terrapins which peered through the marsh grass. Lee finished sketching fortifications, then drew a turtle, including details of the weeds.

When work was suspended because of nature's sultry attack, Lee went home to Virginia. In his dress uniform he called at Arlington. And neighbors began to whisper. There was much envy around hot Virginia that summer.

"For someone who has known the other since

childhood," a pretty belle with long brunette curls
said, "they certainly seem to see each other in a
different light these days."

"He's lonely," a plain girl replied in a soft drawl.
"His mother's been dead such a short time. He's
got nobody to talk to about his loss except Miss
Custis."

"Well, I'd like to talk to him," the beauty
drawled with a little smile.

"Ya'll got to admit Lieutenant Robert E. Lee is
easily the handsomest young man in this state."

"You might say," the brunette said, shaking her
curls, "that Lieutenant Lee is a good catch for any
girl—except Mary Custis."

"Why do you say that?" the plain girl asked.

"Well, she's from an important family.
Her daddy is the grandson of Mrs. George
Washington, and was adopted by President
Washington."

The girls thought back on the history each knew
so well. George Washington Parke Custis had left
Mount Vernon in 1802 when his grandmother
died. He had then built Arlington on the hills
overlooking Alexandria and Washington.

The brunette gave her curls a toss and spoke her
mind. "I hear Mr. Custis doesn't think too much of
Lieutenant Lee as a match for his only child.
Robert doesn't have any money and won't make
any in the army, either."

The plain girl said, "Probably nothing will come
of it, anyway."

Lee ignored the rumors which had begun to stir
about him and Mary Custis.

He found time to visit his cousins while settling
his mother's estate. They went over topics of
interest, especially the things people had said and
written about the late Mrs. Lee. A cousin had a
clipping from the *National Intelligencer*.

Lee read it slowly:

Her death is such as might have been ex-pected of her life—exhibiting the resignation and composure of a practical Christian, con-scious of having faithfully discharged her duties to God and her fellow creatures.

The lieutenant returned to the mud and muck of Cockspur Island when the weather cooled. But Lee hadn't worked long before he was transferred to Fort Monroe in Virginia.

In the spring of 1831 Mary Custis and Lee were sitting in the magnificent mansion with Mr. and Mrs. Custis nearby. Lee was reading aloud when Mary's mother interrupted him.

"I declare, Lieutenant Lee, those Sir Walter Scott kind of novels are enough to make a body tired. Is that why you look a little fatigued? Is Mary making you read too much?"

Lee's dark eyes flickered with a soft light. "Not at all, Mrs. Custis. I never get tired reading to her."

"Just the same, I think you look tired. Mary, why don't you go into the dining room and get some refreshments for Lieutenant Lee? I believe there is some walnut pound cake on the sideboard."

Mary rose and left the room. A moment of silence followed her leaving.

Lee laid down the novel. "Would you pardon me, please?"

Mr. Custis nodded briefly. Mrs. Custis smiled and said, "Of course."

Lee's neat uniform whispered as his long legs swung him down the hall and into the dining room. Mary was just covering the cake as Lee walked up behind her.

He reached out toward the slice she had cut for him. Mary turned, a little startled, and his arm touched her waist. For a moment, his dark eyes looked down into her blue ones.

"Mary," he said softly. "Oh, Mary, I love you! Will you marry me?" Mary accepted.

Near the wedding date Lee obtained some weeks leave from Fort Monroe and took the steamer up the river to Arlington.

The wedding day of June 30, 1831, dawned to a heavy rainfall. Lee began to be a little concerned as the hour for the wedding drew near and the clergyman had not arrived. Mary, of course, was still not in sight, in the tradition of brides. She could not be seen by her groom before the wedding.

Mr. Custis was also concerned. He tried to lessen the tension by showing the lieutenant's army friends the great four-poster bed which his grandmother's husband, George Washington, had slept in. Mr. Custis had brought it from Mount Vernon when he built Arlington.

"That, gentlemen," Mr. Custis said as the army officers followed him out of the bedroom, "is the closet where I keep many of the clothes President Washington wore. I also have the punchbowl which he used to serve guests at Mount Vernon. We're using it today."

One of the officers paused beside a window. "I wonder if it'll ever stop! Look at that! The rain's coming down so hard I can't even see the Potomac."

The others paused to follow his gaze. Mr. Custis shook his head at the downpour. "The vicar will be drenched unless he got a carriage, and I know him—he always prefers horseback."

He cupped his hands against the window and peered intently through the rain. "There he is! Soaking wet! Excuse me, gentlemen; he's going to have some dry clothes before he can unite my daughter in marriage to your comrade in arms!"

Lee waited quietly for the clergyman to get into

some borrowed clothes. Soon a murmur swept the
assembled guests. Lee turned quickly to see the
clergyman entering. He didn't look the part. He
had borrowed Mr. Custis's clothes, and they didn't
fit well. However, only the long sleeves and cuffs
showed from under his robe.

The music began, and twenty-five-year-old Lee
turned to see his twenty-three-year-old bride
appear. Lee's brother, Smith, as best man, lightly
touched the lieutenant's arm as the soloist sang.

Smith's voice whispered sharply in Lee's ear.
"Well, little brother, I'll have to say you picked the
prettiest of all Virginia's belles."

Lee's dark eyes smiled at his brother. Then they
settled on Mary Anne Custis. The clergyman
cleared his throat. In a few minutes, he introduced
the onlookers to Mr. and Mrs. Robert E. Lee.

Lee and his bride toured relatives' homes on a
honeymoon journey before the lieutenant
reported back to Fort Monroe, Virginia. The
young couple had barely settled into their small
apartment when excitement swept through the
little military post.

Mary heard soldiers running. She called to one
who stopped and answered her anxious questions.

"It's a slave revolt, Mrs. Lee! Less than fifty
miles from here. A slave preacher name of Nat
Turner and a few others have turned on their
masters. Killed more than fifty white folks, I hear
tell."

Mrs. Lee was anxious for her husband to return
to the cramped apartment. She questioned him
about his involvement.

"I'm assigned to construction work, Mim," he
said, using one of his pet names for her. "Regular
army troops will go. I understand the insurrection-
ists have taken to the swamps."

"Is it true that the slaves killed white men, women and children?" Mary asked.

"I'm afraid so. About fifty-five altogether, I'm told," Lee said.

Turner was tried and executed, but the incident caused ripples of special activity. The Virginia General Assembly met to examine the issue of slavery and the black man in particular. People formed a group to free slaves in 1801, calling themselves an emancipation society. Some people, abolitionists, began taking slaves in order to set them free. It was obvious that many thinking people were facing the reality of slavery. But nobody could decide what to do about it, so the issue continued to simmer toward a boil.

At the fort, Mary passed the next few months collecting nursery items, and Lee became a father at Fort Monroe on September 16, 1832. Mary gave birth to George Washington Custis Lee. His father had an immediate effect upon the baby, for Mary told a friend, "If he wakes up in the night and cries and Robert speaks to him, he stops immediately."

In November Mrs. Lee took the baby to Arlington to be displayed to his namesake and grandfather. About Thanksgiving, Lee wrote to his wife:

My sweet little boy! What would I give to see him! The house is a perfect desert without him and his Mother and there is no comfort in it. Take good care of him, Molly, and don't let him be spoiled. Direct him in everything and leave nothing to the guidance of his nurse. I am waking all night to hear his sweet little voice and if in the morning I could only feel his little arms around my neck and his dear little heart fluttering against my breast, I should be too happy.

Mrs. Lee obviously didn't like garrison life. She had grown up in a great mansion. But she came back to the tiny apartment at Fort Monroe for short periods. Then she would head again to the spacious home of Arlington.

Lee knew his wife was spoiled. She had been born to direct a great plantation, and being the wife of an army officer was difficult for her. It wasn't until 1832 that Lee was even a full second lieutenant.

In 1834, Lee was reassigned from Fort Monroe to Washington as assistant to the chief of engineers. He tried to rent a place in the city, but ended up living at his in-law's great home.

Every morning Lee left the mansion to ride horseback across the bridge to the Capitol. He left behind the eight-columned front porch which made Arlington House so distinctive. Lee left the mansion for Washington like any commuter, returning nightly on his horse.

Lee's army career moved slowly for a number of years. His second child, Mary Custis, was born in 1835. Mrs. Lee became ill following the birth and was confined to bed for months.

Lee was shocked when he returned from the Great Lakes where he had been ordered to make military surveys. His wife was suddenly reduced to semi-invalidism.

"Molly," Lee said, "why didn't you write me how ill you've been?"

She smiled weakly. "I wrote you that I was ill. There was no point in telling you anything to grieve your mind when you had such pressing assignments."

"Your beautiful hair!" her husband exclaimed.

"It got so tangled that I cut it off," she smiled weakly.

Lee comforted his wife, assuring her that they

would go to some mineral springs where she might recover from her long illness. But when the couple returned from the supposed curing waters, Mrs. Lee was no better. In fact, she was almost like his mother had been most of her life.

A relative who saw Lee at that sad time said, "I never saw a man so changed and so saddened."

Although Mrs. Lee was always in poor health after that, she bore five more children. William Henry Fitzhugh (called Rooney) was born in June 1837. Annie came in 1839, Agnes in 1841. Robert Edward was born in 1843 and named for his father against Lee's wishes. Mildred, the last, was born in 1846.

"The years have been difficult for Lee since his wife's long illness," a military friend said.

"Yes, some people call him moody," said a young officer. "He is not his cheerful, teasing self. He has become more serious—a mature father."

For awhile, Lee considered resigning his commission to take care of his wife and children. He wrestled with the choice of duty to his family and duty to his calling. His own feelings seemed to be that his family yearnings were selfish.

He explained to Mrs. Lee during her illness when she wanted him to come home:

Why do you urge my immediate return, and tempt me in the strongest manner, to endeavor to get excused from the perform- ance of a duty, imposed on me by my pro- fession, for the pure gratification of my private feelings?

When Lee was home he was close and loving to his children and enjoyed romping with them. One of his favorite activities was to get into bed with all of them and read aloud. It was a time of warm happiness for his children to remember always.

Lee set the example in faith by regularly attending church. When he was with his family, they all trooped to the Episcopal Church in which he was reared. Mrs. Lee was often slow in getting ready. Her husband sometimes walked ahead of her because it was against his nature to be tardy.

But Lee's concern with family and church was slowly being pressed into a secondary position. War with Mexico seemed certain. Lee was now a captain.

On May 13, 1846, the United States declared war on her southern neighbor. In August, Lee received orders which sent him to military action.

Chapter 4

Mexican Battlefields Call

At thirty-nine, Lee headed for Mexico sporting a large black mustache, wavy hair combed over the top of his head, and sideburns. Astride his horse he was even more handsome and dignified than ever. His unusually large neck, head and chest made him a striking figure in his uniform when he arrived in Mexico. He was one of 826 officers in the entire United States Army.

It was Lee's duty to fight in Mexico with General Winfield Scott. The major general in charge of American forces had said it was better to fight on foreign soil than American. But the war was not popular with everyone. Some of the officers who fought with Lee in Mexico opposed the war.

Ulysses S. Grant, West Point '43, complained that the troops were "sent to provoke a fight" over political issues. But Grant was a lieutenant, and he obeyed superiors' orders. He was sent across the border as one of the first Americans to invade Mexico.

The Mexicans were ably led by one-legged Santa Ana of Alamo fame. The United States had made Texas a part of the Union although Mexico still claimed the territory. This action was considered a slap in the face to the south-of-the-border authorities. Some Americans considered the war a provoked effort to grab more territory for slave states.

Lee's opinion on slavery was suggested in his will, which he made just prior to entering Mexico. It showed he was worth about $38,750 with few debts. His only slaves, Nancy and her children, were to be freed "soon as it can be done to their advantage and that of others."

Lee had come to Mexico as the duty of an army officer. He did not engage in political side-taking.

Captain Lee had never seen a gun fired in anger until he arrived in Mexico. It was rumored that Santa Ana was going to attack the Americans on Christmas Day. Lee lay in the lazy sun on the grass, his horse saddled and ready. He peered through a telescope watching for the Mexicans. Santa Ana never appeared. While the belated Christmas dinner was finally being prepared, Lee wrote his wife:

"We have had many happy Christmases together. It is the first time we have been entirely separated at this holy time since our marriage." He expressed hope the separation "does not interfere with your happiness, surrounded as you are by father, mother, children, and dear friends." Lee hoped this "is the last time I shall be absent from you during my life." He closed with a reference to his faith: "May God preserve and bless you till then and forever after is my constant prayer."

Lee's horse, Creole, was "full-blooded and considered the prettiest thing in the army." Lee was interested in horses which could be depended upon in military action.

Lee made his first move toward battle when Brigadier General John E. Wool sent him on a scouting mission with a young Mexican. Wool pointed toward the Mexican outside the tent. The general warned, "I don't trust that fellow, Captain Lee. Maybe I can frighten him."

Wool walked to the Mexican. "If you don't bring this man back safely," the general said, pointing to Lee, "I shall hang your father. Understand? *Comprendes?*"

"*Si*, General," the boy said.

The general whispered to Lee, "I still don't trust him. Maybe he plans to do something when I'm not around. Perhaps you should threaten him, too. Threaten him personally."

Lee nodded and produced his pocket pistol. "If you betray me, I shall have to shoot you."

The boy's dark eyes rolled, "*Si, si.*"

Reluctantly, the Mexican youth and the American *soldado* rode into the countryside. The full moon gave them a clear view of objects close up, but distant items were hard to make out. Soon the wagon and mule tracks Lee was following led toward flickering campfires and white, indistinct shapes on a hillside.

"*Capitan!*" the guide's voice sounded frightened. "Look! Santa Ana's troops!"

Lee peered intently into the moonlight. "I'm not sure. Let's get closer."

"No, *por favor!* Please, Capitan! If we are caught, we will be shot or hanged!"

"Just the same," Lee insisted, "I want to get close enough to see their pickets, if that's indeed Santa Ana's encampment."

The guide shook with fright. Lee relented. "Very well. You remain here in silence. I'm going on." He wondered if the boy would run away.

Cautiously, keeping low to the rough ground, Lee made his way down a stream to where the white objects on the hill beyond were clear. Carefully he avoided the cactus. Lee could smell campfires. He also smelled sheep. Clearly he could see sheepherders around the fires and their tents beyond. Captain Lee smiled and walked boldly into the camp. He learned there were no *soldados* around.

Lee returned to his guide, mounted and rode back to give a full and honest report of his findings. If he had turned back with his guide when the white objects were spotted, a false report would have been made.

The captain rested three hours, than led a troop of cavalry to seek Santa Ana's location. On that day, Lee had already ridden forty miles in rough country, but he stayed in the saddle until he located the one-legged enemy leader.

Lee missed the battle action. When he reported his findings, he was reassigned. General Winfield Scott, whom Lee had known in Washington, ordered Lee to place the big guns. The job carried important responsibility for the captain.

Scott was an immense man, fully six feet and five inches tall. He was a little out of condition, overweight, but a capable commander. Scott thought well of Lee and transferred him to what amounted to general staff.

Lee, barely forty years old, reported to Scott on the Brazos where other brilliant soldiers were assembled. The blazing sun beat down on them.

Lee greeted his old friend, Joe Johnston, who had graduated with him from West Point. Lee laughed with Joe over their sailing experiences, recalling Joe had been deathly seasick.

Another soldier Lee met in Mexico was his former West Point friend, Jefferson Davis. He remembered that Jefferson was nearly dismissed. But the rowdy cadet had grown into a competent soldier with colonel's rank. Lee also watched with interest a daring young man named Lieutenant Thomas Jonathan Jackson. He had just graduated the year before.

Other West Point graduates serving in Mexico were Lieutenant D. H. Hill, Jubal Early, Lieuten-

ant George Gordon Meade, brevet lieutenant
George B. McClellan, and Gustavas W. Smith.

Another fine soldier who served with Lee in
Mexico was the dark, handsome Louisianian, First
Lieutenant Pierre G.T. Beauregard. Lee and
Beauregard followed Scott to the low-lying
country of *tierra caliente* (hot land) of Vera Cruz.

The Americans landed without opposition at
the heavily brush-covered open land near the port
city of Vera Cruz. But General Santa Ana was
watching. He had only a light troop of cavalry on
hand to observe the Americans' landing. As it
turned out, Lee and Beauregard were in more
danger from their own men.

On March 19, 1847, Lee and Beauregard were
walking along a narrow trail in thick brush.
Suddenly, an American sentry's nervous challenge
rang out: "Who goes there?"

"Friends!" Lee cried.

"Officers!" Beauregard yelled.

The sentry fired point blank through the brush.
The bullet whizzed between the skin of Lee's
massive upper chest and his arm, within inches of
his heart. But God had spared him.

Firing again rang out on March 24. This time it
was from the enemy. Lee had placed the battery
of guns to answer their fire. For three days, his
men bombarded Vera Cruz's protecting coastal
forts.

The Mexican defenders fired back. Lee wrote
of finding his brother, Smith, during the first day
of bombardment.

No matter where I turned, my eyes re-
verted to him, and I stood by his guns when-
ever I was not wanted elsewhere. Oh! I felt
awfully and am at a loss what I should have
done had he been cut down before me. I
thank God that he was saved. He preserved

his usual cheerfulness, and I could see his
white teeth through all the smoke and din of
fire.

A few days after Vera Cruz surrendered, Lee
was scouting through high brush. Perhaps his
mind was upon the letter he had written home
after the battle: "My heart bled for the inhabitants.
It was awful. The soldiers I did not care so much
for. But it was terrible to think of the women and
children."

Lee suddenly heard voices. Mexican soldiers
were coming through the brush toward him. They
were attracted to a spring in a small clearing. Lee
glanced about for shelter. He dived under a fallen
tree as the soldiers casually came into the open.

For hours, Lee lay still while the soldiers drank
from the spring. They sat on the log where he lay.
Mosquitoes buzzed and flies bit. Lee resisted
insect-slapping and the heat.

When night came, the Mexican troops withdrew
from the spring. Lee carefully crawled out from
under the log and made his way back to his own
lines.

However, Lee had not wasted the day in hiding.
His keen mind had spotted a route for his
engineers to carve a road through the brush
toward Cerro Gordo, the next target town.

Lee was concerned for the village people
involved in the backlash of war. At Vera Cruz,
after the bombardment which he had helped
direct, he came upon a small Mexican drummer
boy with a shattered arm. The boy was trapped
by the weight of a dying Mexican soldier. A little
girl standing by could not move the soldier. The
boy was not strong enough to free his leg.

Lee called to American troops nearby. "Free
the boy. Take the wounded man to medical aid.
See that the boy's arm is treated."

The little girl looked up at the tall American *capitan* with the dark mustache and the soft dark eyes. "*Mil gracias, Senor,*" she said.

Lee wrote Custis, "Her large black eyes were streaming with tears, her hands crossed over her breast; her hair in one long plait behind reached her waist; her shoulders and arms bare and without stockings or shoes."

At Vera Cruz, Lee attended church. Protestants and Catholic Americans alike crowded into the church which had been damaged by guns. Naturally, no English was spoken during the service.

Soldier Henry J. Hunt looked for a place in the crowded church. Captain Lee motioned that there was room beside him and Beauregard. The officer

slipped quietly into place. He saw the unusual
sight of a Protestant general in unfamiliar
surroundings.

An acolyte assisting the priest lighted a large
candle and brought it to General Scott. The
general promptly handed it to Lieutenant
Williams. The acolyte returned with another
candle "not so large or honorable" as the first.
Surprised to see the large, thick candle in a junior
officer's hands, the acolyte blew out the smaller
candle. He returned to the altar and brought
another larger candle to the general who had to
accept it. Eventually, smaller candles were given
all officers.

A side door opened and priests "in gorgeous
vestments" formed a procession. It was obvious
the high-ranking American officers were to be the
honored persons. Hunt's eyes went to Lee, who
had that dignified, quiet appearance habitual to
him, and "looked as if the carrying of candles in
religious processions was an ordinary thing for
him." All the men sighed with relief once outside
the church. The proceeding had been strange to
most of them.

Lee went back to battle. He directed the two-
day bombardment which removed Cerro Gordo
as the last major defensive position between the
Americans and Mexico City.

General Santa Ana barely escaped. He rode
away on a mule with his wooden leg sticking out
stiffly from the animal's side. He dodged between
prickly cactus and rugged rocks.

Lee's letter home told that "My poor Joe
Johnston" had been severely wounded with a ball
in his arm and another above his hip. Lee didn't
mention his own heroic action which brought him
a battlefield promotion to major.

However, old "Fuss and Feathers" Scott

reported on the incidents at Vera Cruz. Lee's strategic placement of guns and effective directing of fire had opened the way to the Mexican capital. Scott wrote:

I am impelled to make special mention of the services of Captain R.E. Lee, Engineers. This officer, greatly distinguished at the siege of Vera Cruz, was again indefatigable, during these operations, in reconnaissance as daring as laborious, and of the utmost value.

Near Mexico City Scott ordered Lee to scout for a way to attack from the rear of the city. Ten thousand Americans were moving toward the capital, but they could see it offered a tremendous challenge if attacked boldly.

The high mountains gave Lee a view of the problem. The Valley of Mexico below was beautiful, with terrible vistas mixed in. There were many lakes and volcanoes, plus a great lava flow. It was this huge broken mass called *pedregal* which challenged the extremely capable Major Lee. The black bubbly mass of hardened lava was treacherous. The sharp lava ripped men's flesh like flinty razors.

Lee was accompanied onto the *pedregal* by another capable officer, Phil Kearney. They scouted enough to see that engineers would have to prepare roads for wagons and artillery. But it was Lee alone who called upon his hardy physical condition to complete the incredible task which lay ahead.

Lee volunteered to carry a message to Scott. Only Lee's keen sense of direction guided him and his small escort through the *pedregal* on the first part of the trip.

A storm came up. Only occasional lightning flashes permitted Lee to determine if he was still going the right direction. The few troopers with

Lee murmured. "If the enemy doesn't kill us," one soldier muttered, "this storm will."

A companion waited for heavy thunder to roll away before answering. "The Mexicans may never get the chance. If you don't keep quiet, our own pickets may shoot us. We're coming to the American outpost."

Lee signaled his presence and walked into the outpost. "Where is General Scott?" he asked.

"He is not here, sir."

Lee's followers groaned. They knew what that meant to Captain Lee. They thought he'd say, "All right, men. Let's cross back and try to find him." But Lee fooled them. He did not ask them to again cross three miles of such slippery, sharp and dangerous terrain.

Lee turned alone into the *pedregal*. He felt his way across the black volcanic rock broken with treacherous holes, chasms and crevasses. Choosing each step with care he jumped yawning abysses after judging the distance by irregular lightning flashes. Lee ignored his cuts, bruises and pains to reach his destination at Zacatepec.

Bleeding, sore and tired, Lee approached the Americans. Standing stiff and wet from the heavy rain, Lee again asked, "Where is General Scott?"

"He has gone back to San Augustin, sir."

There was only one choice for Lee although lesser men would have given up after such a valiant try. Lee again plunged into the *pedregal*. This time, Lee found Scott.

In his command tent General Scott looked at Lee, standing dripping wet and bloody from his repeated crossings of the cruel lava. Scott had sent seven men to get a report on the situation. Each of them had been sent to find General Persifor Smith who was safely across the *pedregal*. Not one of the messengers had gotten through. But Lee, as a

volunteer, had crossed three times in twenty-four hours the lava which a naval officer described as a stormy sea turned to stone.

The information Lee brought Scott allowed the general to mount an attack which was successful. The march on Mexico City was decisive.

Scott called Lee's trips across the *pedregal* "the greatest feat of physical and moral courage performed by any individual, to my knowledge, pending the campaign."

Lee wrote Mary of his excellent physical condition which had made possible his crossing of the lava.

There are few men more healthy or more able to bear exposure and fatigue, nor do I know of any of my present associates that have undergone as much of either in this campaign.

Pushing toward Mexico City, Lee was in the saddle for more than two days and nights. The assault on the hill at Chapultepec was made as Lee directed the cannon fire on September 12, 1847.

All through Saturday and Sunday, Lee rode back and forth to Scott's headquarters after rearranging his batteries. He was on the firing line when casualties were heavy on both sides.

Lee watched as Lieutenant James Longstreet carrying a battle flag fell under enemy fire. George Pickett, only a year out of West Point, snatched up the banner. Wounded Longstreet lay in his own blood at the bottom of a ditch as Lieutenant Pickett carried the flag up to Chapultepec's heights.

Lee stayed in the saddle although he had been fifty hours without sleep. General Scott, seeing the Americans scale the two-hundred-foot-high hill, came upon Lee. The general ordered the major to assist at the San Cosme Gate.

On the way, a bullet struck Lee, inflicting a slight wound. He did not bother to have it dressed. Lee was still in the saddle when General Scott led the Americans up to the Chapultepec terrace. In the excitement, no one noticed Lee's strength draining away with his blood and lack of sleep.

The commanding general didn't see that Lee was still upright only through a tremendous act of willpower. Scott ordered Lee to survey a line of march toward Mexico City.

Lee started forward and carried out his instructions. He returned to Scott and turned his horse to ride alongside the general.

The wounded Lee crumpled from the saddle. He lay in a faint on the heights of Chapultepec and the halls of Montezuma. But his work had earned him the attention of the highest military minds.

Robert E. Lee rode back from Mexico. He reached Washington, D.C., on June 29, 1843. His valorous action at Chapultepec had advanced him another rank, to colonel.

Scott said Lee was the most promising of American soldiers. He added, that since the United States and England again threatened war, "it would be cheap if this country insured the life of Lee at five million dollars a year." Scott had officially reported from Mexico that Lee was "the very best soldier I ever saw in the field."

There were other remarks, less kind, about Scott. "Lee really won the Mexico War and old 'Fuss and Feathers' didn't even need to leave his tent," a young soldier bragged.

But Lee's overwhelming modesty continued to show where his heart was.

"I have much cause for thankfulness and gratitude to that good God who has once more united us," Lee wrote to his brother, Smith.

Lee crossed the Potomac to Arlington to be

reunited with his family. He had been away a long time. He dismounted from his tired horse.

"Where's my little boy?" Lee called, meaning his namesake, Robert Edward Lee. The boy, properly dressed in his best clothing, was present. His golden curls had been combed just right. He watched his father move toward him—then stoop and pick up another boy! Lee had not seen Robert, Jr., in two years. The boy had grown taller so that Lee quite naturally picked up a smaller boy.

Lee's reputation for military strategy brought him a handsome offer to lead an expedition against Spain. Lee refused, saying it was not consistent with his duties to do so. The Cubans who proposed the expedition were later executed with some Americans who got involved in the situation.

Lee's career was advancing. On September 1, 1852, he was appointed superintendent of the military academy where he had graduated twenty-three years before. His oldest son, Custis, was a student there and led his class.

Upon learning of his appointment to West Point, Lee modestly asked the War Department to relieve him of his new responsibility. "I learn with much regret," he wrote, "the determination of the Secretary of War to assign me to that duty, and I fear I cannot realize his expectations in the management of an institution requiring more skill and experience than I can command."

The appointment stood and was made stronger in March 1853 when Jefferson Davis became U.S. Secretary of War. Lee and Davis had known each other since both were cadets, and the war secretary worked well with the new superintendent.

A shattering message arrived at West Point. Mrs. Custis had died unexpectedly. Lee's father-in-law, at seventy-two, was left alone in the great mansion overlooking the Potomac. Lee had grown close to his mother-in-law, and her death seemed to prompt him to take a spiritual step. "She was to me all that a mother could be," Lee said of Mrs. Custis, "and I yield to none in admiration for her character, love for her virtues, and veneration for her memory."

Lee wrote to Martha Custis Williams, one of his wife's cousins, saying: "The blow was so sudden and crushing, that I yet shudder at the shock and feel as if I had been arrested in the course of life and had no power to resume my onward march."

To his wife, Lee wrote: "May God give you strength to enable you to bear and say 'His will be done.' She has gone from all trouble, care and sorrow to a holy immortality, there to rejoice and praise forever the God and Saviour she so long and truly served. May our death be like hers, and may we meet in happiness in heaven." Mrs. Custis's death coupled with Lee's Mexican battle tour moved him deeply.

Something had happened to Lee in Mexico. The reality of death had turned his thoughts more to God. He had been an active churchman all his life. But when he returned from Mexico, he wanted to do something he had never done before: he wanted to be confirmed in his church.

From the time he could understand, Lee had been instructed in the Christian faith. His mother had taught him the catechism before he could read. He had been baptised in the Episcopal Church. He had attended Christ Church in Alexandria. And Lee had been a vestryman of the Episcopal church to help manage Christian affairs. But Lee had never taken a personal step to publicly affirm his beliefs.

On July 17, 1835, during a vacation from his

position at West Point, Lee and his two daughters
knelt together. They became members as they
were confirmed at Christ Church where Lee had
always attended.

The Right Reverend John Johns, Bishop of
Virginia, is supposed to have said, "Colonel Lee, if
you make as valiant a soldier for Christ as you have
made for your country, the church will be as
proud of you as your country now is."

Family ties were strengthened during the thirty-
one months that Lee was superintendent at West
Point. During this time his son Custis graduated as
top man in 1854.

Robert, Jr., told a friend that at West Point his
father often came into his room at night while he
was studying.

Sitting beside his youngest son, the
superintendent "would show me how to
overcome a hard sentence in my Latin reader or a
difficult sum in arithmetic, not by giving me the
translation of the troublesome sentence or the
answer to the sum, but by showing me, step by
step, the way to the right solutions."

The cadets at West Point found that the colonel
was fair but a stern disciplinarian. Some notable
cases came before him, including Philip Henry
Sheridan, '53. Sheridan drew a year's suspension
for attacking a sergeant.

Twice a devoutly religious but fighting
Virginian named James Ewell Brown (J.E.B.)
Stuart came before the superintendent for
disciplinary action. The first time, Jeb Stuart was
involved in a fist fight with four other cadets. Lee
sent the five cadets back to duty after warning
that resorting to fist fighting "is entirely at variance
with the regulations of the academy." The second
time Stuart was summoned before the colonel
there were charges of speaking disrespectfully

to an instructor. Stuart confessed his error, and Lee was "convinced that Cadet Stuart now sees his fault."

His brother's son, Fitzhugh, was twice brought up for disciplinary action for being absent without leave. "Uncle Robert" had no choice but to recommend court-martial. The nephew avoided dismissal when his classmates pledged they would not commit the same offense for a year.

Not all the cadets escaped stern measures when hailed before the colonel. Among those whom Lee dismissed from the academy was James McNeil Whistler. He later became famous as the painter of a portrait the art world still calls, "Whistler's Mother."

Lee tired of West Point after nearly three years. Secretary of War Jefferson Davis learned of Lee's restlessness and proposed a change.

Americans were pouring West to fill the vast lands clear to California, where gold had been discovered in 1848. Immigrants swarming across traditional Indian grounds were running into scalping parties. Outlaws operating along the Mexican border were robbing and burning. And there weren't enough qualified cavalrymen. Would Lee like to be transferred to the West?

It meant leaving the engineers where he had been since graduating as a cadet twenty-six years before. But it also meant possible faster promotions. Besides, Lee was a natural horseman since his father had lifted him onto a gentle mare over forty years before. Lee accepted the new challenge.

As a lieutenant colonel under Colonel Albert Sidney Johnston, Lee joined the Second Cavalry. The unit was newly created for the western frontier.

The important document which Lee signed on March 15, 1855, reads:

I, Robert E. Lee, appointed a Lieutenant Colonel in the Second Regt. of Cavalry in the Army of the United States, do solemnly swear, or affirm, that I will bear true allegiance to the United States of America, and that I will serve them honestly and faithfully against all their enemies or oppressors whatsoever; and observe and obey the orders of the President of the United States . . .

It was an oath of allegiance that later caused a problem in the life of Robert E. Lee.

Chapter 5

War in the Winds

Lee spent his first summer on the western plains in a hot tent pitched at Camp Cooper, West Texas. It was a lonely life. Lee could not even find a cat to help guard his seven chickens he had brought along in a coop. There were plenty of rattlesnakes, many tarantulas and other unwelcome creatures.

The only break in the dull routine of keeping an eye on Comanche Indians was occasional court-martial duty. Lee had done some of that on the way to his dreary post.

A friend from academy days was there, John B. Hood. He sometimes rode with the colonel across the wilderness. Hood came riding back into camp one day with his left hand pinned to the saddle by an Indian arrow. Four of the cavalrymen that had been with him were wounded and two killed.

But while in Texas, Lee never got a scratch.
There were distant sounds of violent conflict.
There were newspapers for Lee to read with
accounts of hot arguments between abolitionists
and slave supporting groups. There were small-
scale flare-ups in various places, all sounding
faintly like a gathering storm.

Barely eighty years before, there had been
thirteen colonies which united to win a war against
England's King George III. Some people believed
the years since then had proved the states should
function as one union. Others, not believing there
was any need for the states to be solidly unified,
felt that each state could work alone, and that the
government was made up of a free association of
states.

Among these "states righters" was South
Carolina, which had made noises about going her
own way for years. The sounds of battle over
states' rights and slavery were building up.

Lee had read about the Know-Nothing party
and the Free-Soilers. He knew about Free States
and Slave States.

His Christmas letter to Mary included
references to President Franklin Pierce's annual
message to Congress and a report by the secretary
of war. Lee told his wife:

"In this enlightened age, there are few, I believe,
but what will acknowledge that slavery as an
institution is a moral and political evil in any
country." Slavery was a greater evil to the white
man than the black, Lee continued. His feelings
were "strongly enlisted" on the black man's side,
but "my sympathies are more strong" with the
whites.

He thought the blacks' "emancipation will
sooner result from the mild and melting influence

of Christianity than the storms and tempests of firey controversy."

Lee admitted that only a small part of the human race had been converted to "the doctrines and miracles of our Saviour" in two thousand years, but the results must be left "in His hands who sees the end; who chooses to work by slow influences; and with whom two thousand years is but as a single day."

Lee did not approve of slavery, and he saw that "the course of the final abolition of human slavery is onward," but men could only pray, use "all justifiable means in our power" and trust God to work out the end.

Distant rumblings of war were being heard. But Lee had family problems. His "baby" sister Mildred, now married, died at age forty-five. Lee had not expected "that she might precede me on the unexplored journey upon which we are hastening."

He added that, "I pray that her life has but just begun, and I trust that our merciful God only so suddenly and early snatched her away because He saw that it was the fittest moment to take her to Himself. May a pure and eternal life be hers, and may we all live so that when we die, it may be open to us."

Lee would be absent from them at the sacred season but "I trust many of you will be assembled around the family hearth at dear Arlington another Christmas." His "heart will be in the midst of you, and I shall enjoy in imagination and memory all that is going on . . ."

He added a political observation: "Mr. Buchanan, it appears, is to be our next President. I hope he will be able to extinguish fanaticism North and South, cultivate love for the country and Union, and restore harmony between the different factions."

Lee's companions on the frontier encountered Indians and had bloody skirmishes. But the colonel's life was mostly wrapped up in dull court-martials and lonely, harsh line duty.

At Easter 1857, Lee remembered the meaning of the holy time. He was on a post without a church. His services, that day, he wrote "have been performed alone in my tent, I hope with a humble, grateful and penitent heart, and will be acceptable to our Heavenly Father."

The colonel's career took a sudden swerve in October when word reached Lee that his father-in-law had died. Arlington's affairs were in a tangled mess. Lee applied for a two-month's leave of absence and went home to Virginia.

Lee arrived to find his wife in very poor physical condition. Her feet and ankles were painfully swollen. Her right arm was crippled, and she could hardly walk. Like Lee's mother, his wife was an invalid.

Under the terms of the will, George Washington Parke Custis had left Lee's wife the great mansion and several slaves. Said Lee of the slaves, Custis "has left me an unpleasant legacy."

Lee's position on slavery was already known. His will had specified freedom for his few slaves. He had allowed other slaves to sail to Nigeria. Now he had his father-in-law's slaves to handle for a few years. Under the old gentleman's will they were to be freed within five years.

Bitterness over slavery boiled over onto the colonel on June 24, 1859. The first of two unsigned letters was published in the *New York Tribune*. The writer claimed to be Lee's neighbor, but it was obvious the person did not have all the facts about Custis's will. It was also obvious that the writer did not really know Robert E. Lee.

"All the slaves on this estate, as I understand," the letter ran, "were set free at the death of Custis, but are now held in bondage by Lee." The letter said that two men and a woman slave had run away but were caught by an officer and returned. "Col. Lee ordered them whipped," the letter writer continued. "The officer whipped the two men, and said he would not whip the woman, and Col. Lee stripped her and whipped her himself." These were "facts as I learn from near relatives and the men whipped," the first letter concluded. Admittedly, information was not first-hand.

Two days later, the second unsigned poison-pen letter in the Northern newspaper repeated the story.

Lee and those who knew him were aware that he was not capable of doing such a thing. Still, he didn't defend himself. He wrote his son, Custis that "the *N.Y. Tribune* has attacked me for my treatment of your grandfather's legacy, but I shall not reply."

The personal slavery issue was another and faster beat in the drum roll of history, bringing nearer and louder the clash of Civil War. Lee had said in his letter to his wife in December 1856 that "efforts of certain people of the North, to interfere with the domestic institutions of the South," were "both unlawful and entirely foreign . . ." and "can only be accomplished by them through the agency of a Civil and Servile war."

That terrible prophecy came closer when Lee was ordered to Washington. He listened to a briefing on a mysterious attack on a U.S. military arsenal in Virginia.

In a way, Virginia had been invaded. The first spark of the Civil War flared.

Lee learned that a group of men had seized the federal arsenal. His orders were to put down the rebellion at Harper's Ferry.

Jeb Stuart and Lieutenant Green accompanied Colonel Lee and his troops to the scene. A "Mr. Smith" had holed up inside a fire-engine house with some slaves and hostages.

Lee suspected the group's leader was John Brown, who was violently against slavery. He had

already caused much trouble in Kansas. Only
Stuart had ever seen Brown. Lee sent Stuart to
read a surrender demand at the engine-room door.

The plan was that Lee would wait for a signal
from the cavalryman which meant the talk had
failed. Commander Lee would then order his
twelve men to attack.

"I approached the door in the presence of
perhaps two thousand spectators," Stuart
explained, "and told Mr. Smith that I had a
communication for him from Colonel Lee."

The leader of the rebel band opened the door
about four inches. He placed his body against the
opening and held a cocked carbine on the young
lieutenant. Stuart recognized the small, wiry man
with gray eyes. Yes, the grizzled beard and hair
belonged to "Osawatomie Brown." He was the
troublemaker.

Some of the hostages begged for Colonel Lee to
come and see Brown. Stuart told them Lee would
accept only prompt surrender.

Brown refused. Lieutenant Stuart moved back
from the door and slowly waved his hat in the air
as the attack signal.

Lee ordered the storming party to the door with
hammers. In his official report, Lee said "the doors
were fastened by ropes, the spring of which
prevented their being broken by the hammers."

The troops led by Lieutenant Green dropped
the hammers and began using a ladder as a
battering ram. A man fell mortally wounded from
gunfire. Inside the engine-room others were dying
or wounded.

A ragged hole was punched through the engine-
house door. Lieutenant Green said he "instantly
stepped from my position" and entered the hole
made by the ladder. One of the hostages, Colonel
Lewis W. Washington (a relative of the late

president), pointed Brown out to the officer. Immediately Green attacked Brown with his light dress sword, taking him prisoner.

Lee reported the incident was over in a few minutes. But the event at Harper's Ferry was not really over—not at all. And, without realizing it, Lee had become involved in the bloodshed of what was to become an explosive spark to the Civil War.

Brown had called for a slave uprising. Only the five black men and sixteen white men with him had risen to his call. But Virginians were nervous, remembering the Nat Turner episode. Lee also remembered the Turner uprising. He had been a young engineer at nearby Fort Monroe when that happened.

On December 2, 1859, about six weeks after Lee's troops recaptured the federal arsenal at Harper's Ferry, John Brown was hanged. But, as a song was soon to say, "John Brown's body lies a'mouldering in the grave, but his soul goes marching on."

Lee gave Brown very little attention outside of his official reports. He barely mentioned the man in letters to his family and friends.

But the North gave Brown much space in newspapers. This was fanned into a fire when it was learned that prominent Northerners had backed the troublemaker.

Brown was hailed as a martyr by abolitionists. Revenge for his death was threatened. In a prophetic note given to a spectator as he was brought out of jail for his hanging, Brown wrote he was "now quite certain that the crimes of this guilty land" would "never be purged away; but with blood."

Brown's action at Harper's Ferry had torn the country farther apart. More citizens were forced

to line up for or against states' rights and slavery.
But Lee, always aloof to non-military matters,
returned to duty as the career soldier he was.

In February 1860 he took a railroad trip to New
Orleans on his way to San Antonio, Texas. His
friend Beauregard lived nearby.

The cavalry commander got some futile
exercise in Texas. He chased bandit Juan Cortinas
when he raided north of the border. He was so
hard to catch that Lee called him "that myth
Cortinas."

The rest of 1860 went rapidly, with several
events occurring for Lee to remember. Rooney
made Lee a grandfather. The boy was named
after Lee, who wrote, "I wish I could offer him a
more worthy name and a better example."

Joe Johnston, Lee's friend from West Point, was
promoted to quartermaster general and given the
rank of a brigadier. Lee had been one of four men
considered for the post. But he remained a cavalry
colonel chasing a mythical man who raided
border towns.

Lee sent a letter to his old friend, saluting him
with his new rank: "My Dear General: I am
delighted . . . by your present title, and I feel my
heart exult within me at your high position."

Lee blamed himself for "errors" he had made
which caused him to be passed over for
promotion. However, he was now the highest
ranking officer in Texas.

The biggest national news that year reached Lee
around Thanksgiving. Abraham Lincoln had been
elected President, and everyone knew he was
against slavery.

All around him, Lee heard angry Texans
declare, "Texas should get out of the Union. We
won't take Lincoln in the White House."

But it was South Carolina which showed how

very strongly the South felt about Lincoln's election. South Carolina called for a convention to consider withdrawing from the Union.

Lee penned a note to his son. "The Southern States seem to be in a convulsion." He told Custis, "It is difficult to see what will be the result, but I hope all will end well."

Lee was hopeful "for the preservation of the Union." He said, "I am not pleased with the course of the Cotton States." "While I wish to do what is right, I am unwilling to do what is wrong, either at the bidding of the South or the North," he explained. Of the South's plan to renew the slave trade, he said, "I am opposed to it on every ground."

Lee had been cautious and said little about his views while in Texas. As a military man, his opinion was best kept to himself.

However, when Dr. Willis G. Edwards asked if a man's first allegiance is to his state or the nation, Lee had a prompt answer.

"My loyalty to Virginia ought to take precedence over what is due the Federal government," Lee replied.

"If Virginia stands by the Union," he had announced earlier, "so will I. But if she secedes (although I do not believe in secession as a Constitutional right, nor is there sufficient cause for revolution) then I will follow my native state with my sword, and if need be, with my life."

A woman in the Read House, the hotel where Lee was staying, told a friend about the troubled cavalryman. "He returned at night and shut himself in his room, which was over mine, and I heard his footsteps through the night, and sometimes the murmur of his voice, as if he were praying," she said.

Lee told a fellow army officer, "When I get to

Virginia, I think the world will have one soldier less. I shall resign and go to planting corn." Lee packed his belongings and headed for Washington.

Three days after Lee reached his destination, Lincoln took the oath of office. And Lee reported to General Scott in the Capitol. What the seventy-five-year-old Scott said to the fifty-five-year-old colonel was never revealed by Lee or Scott. But we may surmise.

Since Lincoln had been elected in the previous autumn, the issue of states' rights versus the Union had raged across the land. The main issue was not slavery, but whether a federation of states which had banded together in the Revolution could be forced to stay together at the command of a central government.

The Revolution was not that far in the past. Most men felt a loyalty to their states. The question of having to make a choice between state and Union was new.

Some, like Lee, had already expressed themselves. But Lee was still in the United States Army. He was still under the oath of allegiance he had signed when he switched from the engineers to the cavalry upon leaving the superintendency at West Point.

The talk between Scott and Lee might have been about the rapid turn of events which had followed Lincoln's election. Three months ago South Carolina had left the Union. Mississippi had seceded on January 11. The next day, Florida quit the Union, with Alabama following the next day. Georgia went out on January 19, trailed by Louisiana on January 26 and Texas on February 23.

Still, most people did not believe war would

result. Or, it was argued, if it did come to that, it would be a short war.

Whether the old general and Lee talked of these matters that March day in 1861 is speculation. Some people say that Scott offered Lee command of all Union forces, or at least an opportunity to be promoted to general. Lee left the commanding general's office and never revealed what was said, and Scott was equally closed mouthed.

But Mrs. Lee, then so crippled she was confined to a rolling chair, was more frank. "My husband was summoned to Washington where every motive and argument was used to induce him to accept the command of the army destined to invade the South," she wrote a friend.

Before the month was up, Lee was offered the rank of brigadier general in the Confederate government's new army being raised in Montgomery, Alabama. Lee simply ignored the offer. About the same time, President Lincoln signed a new commission advancing Lee to full colonel, up from the brevet colonel rank.

It was a difficult time for Lee, a Southerner and sixth generation Virginian.

It was the gunners at Charlestown Harbor who forced Robert E. Lee to make the toughest decision of his life. For, on April 12, the United States, as the Union, was fired upon by Confederate gunners.

The Civil War began with the first cannon roar at Fort Sumter.

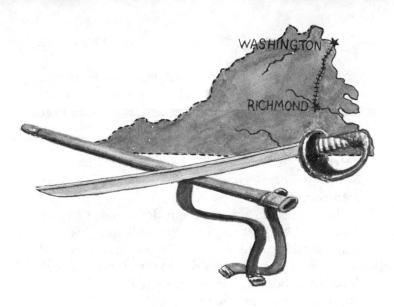

Chapter 6

A Sword for Virginia

Lee's military buddy P.G.T. Beauregard was commander of the Confederate States of America's batteries in South Carolina. He had ordered the first shot at Fort Sumter.

After two days of Confederate guns firing on Fort Sumter, the federal post surrendered. Nobody had been killed on either side. But the American flag had been fired upon.

On April 15, 1861, President Lincoln issued a call for states to furnish 75,000 troops to "suppress combinations" and to "cause the laws to be duly executed."

Northern states and Virginia, North Carolina, Tennessee and Arkansas would have to send troops to fight against their friends, relatives and neighbors—if these states stayed in the Union.

Virginia's legislative body met secretly on April 17 to discuss what to do. Should Virginia remain in the Union?

On April 18 Lee arose and dressed at Arlington.
He shaved, seeing his reflection—a fifty-four-
year-old man in wonderful physical condition.
Mary watched her husband with admiring eyes.
He wore a black mustache as he had when superintendent of West Point. His wavy dark hair was
showing some gray, but he was still a very
handsome man.

Two messages had been delivered the day
before. One asked Lee to call on his old
commander again. General Scott obviously had
something important to discuss with the colonel.
The other note was from Francis P. Blair, Sr., an
important man in Washington.

Lee mounted and rode down from the rolling
hills of Arlington, past the wild flowers beginning
to bloom and across the Potomac River. The
horse's hoofs beat a drum-like military roll across
the bridge. Lee moved along Pennsylvania
Avenue to the Blair House, directly across the
street from the White House.

Blair and Lee had met before. The host was
former editor of *The Congressional Globe*.

Blair came right to the point. He had been to see
President Lincoln. There was an indication Lee
could become commanding general of the
massive new Union army being raised.

Later Lee reported, "I never intimated to any
one that I desired the command of the United
States Army; nor did I ever have a conversation
with but one gentleman, Mr. Francis Preston Blair,
on the subject, which was at his invitation, and, as I
understood, at the instance of President Lincoln.
After listening to his remarks, I declined the offer
he made me, to take command of the
army . . . I could take no part in an invasion of
the Southern states."

Lee's position was clear. He left Blair and went

to the State, War and Navy Building. General
Scott received Lee with a serious face.

Lee told his commander what he had said to
Blair. The old soldier shook his head. Scott was
obviously deeply moved.

"Lee, you have made the greatest mistake of
your life." The huge general, slowed by age
paused, then added, "But I feared it would be so."

It was a hard moment for both men. Lee was
known to be the general's favorite soldier. They
had known each other well from trying days in
Mexico. They had been good friends since then.
But now the situation erased any possibility of this
relationship continuing.

Scott is reported to have added, "There are
times when every officer in the United States
service should fully determine what course he will
pursue and frankly declare it."

Heaving his bulk out of the chair, the general
said, "I suppose you will go with the rest. If you
propose to resign, it is better that you should do so
at once."

Lee understood. If orders came to the United
States Army to move against the rebels, it would
be Lee's duty to obey. He was a part of that U.S.
Army. He had signed an oath of allegiance.

A third call was made before Lee left the
capital. He stopped to see his brother, Smith,
stationed with the navy in Washington. They
talked of the problems.

Lee thought about his family that had been in
Virginia for eight generations. All around Virginia
there were Lee cousins, aunts, uncles. The great
plantations had known generations of Lees. The
churches had heard the voices of untold Lee
family members raising their voices in praise, for
they were a God-fearing people. All across
Virginia, now fresh with new grass and swelling

buds, tombstones marked the final resting places of the Lees. But, more importantly, all over the landscape were living relatives who bore the Lee name, or were close blood kin.

The colonel ended the meeting with his brother, saying he would contact Smith again in a few days. Lee mounted and rode toward home.

Arlington House lay squarely in the path of any Northern invasion of Virginia. The military man in Lee knew there was no way of defending the family plantation if Lincoln ordered troops across the Potomac.

The big question was: would Virginia join the other states in withdrawing from the Union? The people had until May 23 to decide. But Lee had to make his decision at once: to stay in the U.S. Army and fight his state, his family, his friends; or to resign his commission.

The next day brought the necessity for a decision to a head. Lee rode into Alexandria on April 19. The city was crackling with excitement. Lee watched the waving of banners with his usual quiet reserve. He went into the Stabler-Leadbeater Apothecary shop to pay a bill.

Someone asked, "Colonel Lee, what do you think of Virginia's decision to secede, subject to the vote of the people on May 23?"

Lee replied quietly, "I must say that I am one of those dull creatures that cannot see the good of secession."

The druggist marked Lee's bill "paid," then scrawled Lee's remarks about secession on the corner of the ledger.

The colonel walked outside into the warm spring air. The streets of the town where he had grown up were noiser than before. He caught the temper of his fellow Virginians in their loud remarks.

"We're going to have to fight; that's for sure," a gray-haired man shouted.

"Let the war come! It won't last long!" his son stormed.

"That's right!" their friend on horseback laughed. "The South'll whip them Yankees before they know'd what happened!"

"You're right! Absolutely right! The war won't last long; a few months at the most," the father said.

Lee's military experience told him this was impossible. If war came, it would not be brief. It would be long, bloody and painful. He remembered the Mexican battlefields. War would hurt, and war would personally hurt him, for he had much to lose.

Lee returned to Arlington with a copy of the *Alexandria Gazette*. He handed it to his wife without saying a word. Mrs. Lee only needed a glance to understand. By a two to one vote, the Virginia Convention had voted to secede. Ratification by the people was now merely a form. Virginia had made her choice.

Now Lee must make his. He told his wife he wanted to be left alone. He climbed the stairs in the mansion.

Mrs. Lee could hear her husband pacing upstairs. Far into the dark hours of that warm April evening she heard his measured footfalls. Sometimes he fell to his knees, and Mrs. Lee knew he was praying for divine guidance. Should he resign his command in the U.S. Army he had sworn to uphold against all enemies?

From his window on the second floor, Lee could see across the Potomac. He could see the flickering lights which marked the Capitol.

It was near midnight when Mrs. Lee heard her husband stop pacing again. But she did not hear

his knees on the floor. Instead, a chair scraped
faintly as though he had pulled the one away from
his desk. Mrs. Lee correctly guessed that her
husband was writing letters.

Lee had made his decision.

It was well after midnight when Lee came
downstairs with some letters in his hands. He
approached his wife in her wheelchair and handed
her the letters without speaking.

She read the first one to the secretary of war. It
was brief:

> *Sir—I have the honor to tender the resigna-
> tion of my Commission as Colonel of the lst
> Regt of Cavalry.*

The second letter to General Scott, long-time
friend and military comrade, was longer. But it
began bluntly, with the tone which indicated how
things had changed in a few days.

"General," Lee wrote, "Since my interview with
you on the 18th inst. I have felt that I ought no
longer to retain my commission in the
Army . . . therefore tender my resignation, which
I request you will recommend for acceptance."

Lee added, "It would have been presented at
once but for the struggle it cost me to separate
myself from a service to which I have devoted the
best years of my life and all the ability I
possessed."

Since Lee was eighteen years old, he had turned
his whole life to the military. Now, on April 20,
1861, long before dawn, Lee thanked General
Scott for his "kindness and consideration." Lee
said he would remember the rest of his life the
good memories of the general.

"Save in the defense of my native state," Lee
concluded, "I never desire again to draw my
sword."

It took a few days for the letter to be officially

noted in the War Department. On April 25, the secretary of war's signature and the word, "accepted," showed it was final. After thirty-two years, Lee's service to the U.S. Army had ended.

Lee wrote another letter to explain to his brother, Smith, that he had resigned.

"I wished to wait until the Ordinance of Secession should be acted on by the people of Virginia," Lee wrote, "but war seems to have commenced, and I am liable at any time to be ordered on duty which I could not conscientiously perform. To save me from such a position, and to prevent the necessity of resigning under orders, I had to act at once . . ."

He was, Lee concluded, "now a private citizen, and have no other ambition than to remain at home . . ."

Lee's letter to his sister, Anne, was difficult. Her son was in the U.S. Army and her husband was for the North. To her, Lee explained his resignation.

"I have not been able to make up my mind to raise my hand against my relatives, my children, my home." He said that "save in defense of my native state (with the sincere hope that my poor services may never be needed), I hope I may never be called on to draw my sword."

That Saturday morning the *Alexandria Gazette* had an editorial about Lee. "It is probable that the secession of Virginia will cause an immediate resignation of many officers of the Army and Navy from this State. We do not know, and have no right to speak for or anticipate the course of Colonel Robert E. Lee. Whatever he may do, will be conscientious and honorable."

But, the newspaper continued, if Lee did resign, "there is no man more worthy to head our forces and lead our army."

The editorial gave further praise to Lee as a

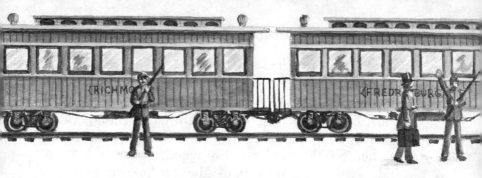

soldier in whom the people of Virginia had confidence, noting "his Christian life and conduct" make his name a "tower of strength."

Mrs. Lee wrote to a friend, "My husband has wept tears of blood over this terrible war, but as a man of honor and a Virginian, he must follow the destiny of his State."

Lee went to Christ Church in Alexandria the next day where three strangers talked to him in the courtyard. The governor was summoning Lee to a meeting.

On Monday Lee left Arlington for the last time in his life and headed for Richmond, capital of Virginia.

Lee had much to think about as the train rattled and swayed south to Richmond. Dressed as a civilian, Lee looked out the window at the passing countryside. The sky was clear; the weather warm for April. In Arlington the yellow jessamine was not quite in full bloom. Further south it turned lawns gold. Lee admired the dogwood. Apple blossoms were dressing the trees with pastels. Cardinals flickered red bodies across the flowering trees and budding shrubs. Lee, the soldier, sighed. He felt that Union troops would soon be tramping down the spring flowers, and the boom of guns would send the birds from their nests and still their songs.

On and on the train clicked, passing freshly plowed red clay fields, and stopping now and then for excited passengers. The train hissed to a

stop at Manassas Junction. Then the engineer blew
the whistle; the train jerked and slowly moved off
in a heavy black cloud of smoke.

Lee reached Richmond on April 22 and took a
carriage to the Spotswood Hotel. He went to his
room, aware of the shrill babble of voices around
him, yet serene as a rock in the middle of a
turbulent river.

"Did you ever see so many handsome young
men?" a pretty woman gushed to her blonde
girlfriend. "I declare, Richmond never had so
many men in so many fine uniforms. Why, I just
saw cadets from Virginia Military Institute. Even
their officer is a fine looking man. I heard his name
is Major Thomas Jonathan Jackson."

"You know what, Mary Belle? I hear the boys
from Georgia are wearing homemade jackets!
Imagine!" The blonde bubbled. "And those
Texans, with their quaint western clothes and their
hair so long. Why, I even saw some drummers
with red jackets, marching along at the head of a
column . . ."

Lee walked out of hearing. He had seen the
volunteers, pouring into Richmond with every
train, anxious to fight and win glory. Lee sighed. It
wasn't going to be like that.

It was going to be bloody and bitter, and the
hurt would not go away for a long time. Now these
men needed organization to be ready for the
invasion which would come, perhaps on May 5.
That was the day Lincoln had set as the deadline
when his proclamation ordered rebels to "disperse
and retire peaceably . . . within twenty days."

Civilian Lee was prepared to meet Virginia's
Governor John Letche. Officially, Lee had not
received notice his United States Army resignation had been accepted, but it was naturally

expected it would be. So Lee cleaned up after the train ride and presented himself to the governor.

The governor's mansion, next door to the capitol of Virginia, was just down the block from the Spotswood Hotel. Lee walked through the crowded streets, alive with banners, colorful uniforms and marching feet.

Music filled the air; bright, expectant martial music. One piece was like a minstrel song. Lee had not heard it before. Someone in the hotel lobby had commented that this new tune was called "*Dixie.*"

Governor Letche explained the reason he had called Lee to Richmond. The state convention had authorized appointment of a "commander of the military and naval forces of Virginia." The position carried the rank of major general. Lee had been recommended. Did he want the responsibility?

It was time for another decision. Virginia was an independent state, obviously out of the Union but not yet joined with the Confederate States of America (CSA).

With typical modesty, Lee accepted. He asked that it be noted he had already tendered his resignation from the United States Army before Virginia had called him. He knew there would be those who claimed he had betrayed his first command for the higher rank in his mother state. But Lee had known nothing of the new rank until the governor offered it.

Lee was back in uniform again, but this one was gray—not blue. He arose early on Tuesday to open his office. He didn't have anyone to help, but Lee began preparations for molding Virginia's naval and land forces into fighting shape.

The CSA had its capital at Montgomery,

Alabama. A representative was rumored in
Richmond, apparently to suggest Virginia join the
Confederates.

Lee drafted his General Order No.1,
announcing he had assumed command of
Virginia's military and naval forces.

Outside his office he could see the wide
assortment of flags and banners flying. There
were some homemade flags, and many South
Carolina flags showing a single star and called the
Bonnie Blue flag. The Confederacy had no single
flag.

A committee came to Lee's office and escorted
him to the capitol where word of his acceptance
had gone ahead of him. The Virginia state
convention rose in a standing ovation as Lee
entered the chamber.

John Janney, president of the convention, made
the solemn remarks. "Sir, we have, by this
unanimous vote, expressed our conviction that
you are at this day, among the living citizens of
Virginia, 'first in war.' "

It was an obvious reference to Lee's father's
words about George Washington, "first in war,
first in peace and first in the hearts of his
countrymen."

Janney continued addressing Lee before the
convention. "We pray God most fervently that
you may so conduct the operations committed to
your charge, that it will soon be said of you, that
you are 'first in peace,' and when that time comes
you will have earned the still prouder distinction
of being 'first in the hearts of your countrymen.' "

Lee was dignified, but embarrassed. He was not
used to such public praise. But the president was
hurrying on. "Yesterday, your mother, Virginia,
placed her sword in your hand . . . that you will
draw it only in her defense, and that you will fall

with it in your hand rather than the object for which it was placed there, shall fail."

Lee said, "Trusting to Almighty God, an approving conscience, and the aid of my fellow citizens, I will devote myself to the defense and service of my native state, in whose behalf alone would I have ever drawn my sword."

Lee retired from the unaccustomed public acclaim as soon as possible. He went about his business of preparing for a possible invasion, knowing how helpless the situation really was.

The twenty-one Union states had more than twenty-three million total residents. Counting slaves, the eleven Southern states had a population of only nine million. The North had factories to make guns, uniforms, boots. They had railroads, shipping and plenty of money. The South was a land of farmers without naval or military supplies and little money to buy them.

Lee knew about Virginia too. At its widest part the state was 425 miles wide. Protecting Virginia would be nearly an impossible job, but it might be done with tremendous work. Lee was forced to throw all his years of experience into a rushed organizational effort.

Lee worked late. When he retired to his hotel, a visitor was waiting to see him, Alexander H. Stephens, vice-president of the new Confederate States of America. He had first seen Lee in front of the Virginia Convention that morning. Lee and Stephens talked briefly about the problems involved with Virginia's joining CSA.

Lee, now major general of Virginia's forces, hurried through the next several days, preparing for Lincoln's deadline.

Lee soberly read the supply reports coming in to Richmond: 60,000 small arms, another 54,000 flintlocks; hardly the kind of weapons to win

battles against the mighty North. In 1861, Union
troops were issued over one million firearms.
Virginia's volunteers had only forty-six thousand.

Virginia asked her citizens to equip volunteers
with clothing. There weren't enough uniforms for
the anxious men and boys signing up. Lee, looking
out his window at the troops practicing marching
on the streets of Richmond, saw some were boys
not over fourteen years of age.

In the midst of his crushing schedule, Lee took
time to write his wife. "War is inevitable," he
wrote in his first letter five days after arriving in
Richmond, "and there is no telling when it will
burst around you."

He urged her to flee Arlington and find a safe
place. He concluded, "May God keep and
preserve you and have mercy on all our people."

The days allowed by Lincoln for the rebel states
to disband rushed by. Lee worked calmly and
efficiently to be ready. The May 5 deadline came
and went. Lee did not hear the tramp of Union
troops, but he feared the sound would soon reach
Virginians.

He kept working. He reviewed his best officers'
strengths and tried to decide where the Union
would hit first. Lee was cheered by the presence
of Thomas J. Jackson. He had left his position as
artillery instructor at V.M.I. and arrived in
Richmond with cadets from his classes who were
to help defend the capital.

By May 14, with Virginia in the Confederacy,
Lee was nominated to be a brigadier general,
along with his old West Point friend Joe Johnston.
Beauregard was now a general, too. They were
tested, trusted and tremendous fighting men.

Where would the Union strike? The
Confederacy had no dependable spy system. But

indications were that the blue-coated soldiers would hit a vital railroad junction, such as Manassas.

The volunteers continued to come from many Southern states, for it was logical Virginia would be attacked first. Her borders touched the North. Some soldiers had come without weapons, expecting Virginia to supply them. Some were handsomely dressed in fancy uniforms while others wore gray homespun.

Lee's letters continued to reach his wife. He sent one in May to Mrs. Lee in care of his cousin at Ravensworth. He figured Mrs. Lee had fled Arlington, but she had not.

He replied to her letter at once, urging her to flee, but being careful not to alarm her. "I am glad to hear you are . . . enjoying the sweet weather and beautiful flowers," he began. He suggested she "retire further from the scene of war."

The day after Virginia formally approved the Ordinance of Secession, Union troops struck across the Potomac, overrunning Arlington at once. Trenches were promptly dug in the graceful lawn. Mrs. Lee had fled to Ravensworth.

Thirteen thousand blue-clad troopers were spreading into Virginia. Major General Charles W. Sanford ordered his troops to pitch camp behind the Arlington mansion.

Once the Federals marched into battle, other events happened rapidly. President Jefferson Davis moved to Richmond where the Confederacy's capital was relocated from Alabama.

Battles were small until July 17. As Lee had guessed, the Union troops hit in force at Manassas Junction. Pierre Beauregard sent a message to Richmond.

He was under heavy attack and falling back
to Bull Run, a near-by creek. He needed reinforcements at once.

Thomas J. Jackson was ordered up with his few
thousand men. The battle continued with
indications that the South was losing badly.

On July 21, President Davis boarded a special
train to inspect the scene. Lee wanted to go, but he
was bound by his president's orders to stay in
Richmond. Anxiously, Lee waited, "mortified"
that he had no troops to lead at the defenses he had
planned.

Finally, word came from Manassas.

Chapter 7

Rebel Yell

Richmond was tense after the five days of hard fighting at Manassas. Rumors were flying.

"Beauregard and Johnston have been thrown back. The North is winning a major victory," an old gentleman cried.

"Yes, I know. I know," a friend said softly. "And my son is there."

Lee held himself apart from the tense crowds around the Spotswood Hotel. A telegram came and Lee heard shouting in the streets. He learned that President Davis had wired, date line July 21, 1861:

We have won a glorious though dear-bought victory. Night closed on the enemy in full flight and closely pursued.

The crowded streets of Richmond went wild. The South had won a major victory in the first important battle.

Lee soon found that Davis's telegram was not
fully correct. The enemy had not been pursued.
The Confederates could have pushed right into
Washington, but they did not.

Lee showed his bigness of heart by wiring
Beauregard, "I cannot express the joy I feel at the
brilliant victory of the 21st. The skill, courage and
endurance displayed by yourself excites my
highest admiration."

Congratulations were also in order for another
old Lee friend, Thomas J. Jackson. He had picked
up a proud nickname at Manassas. Lee heard the
story as it went the rounds of Richmond.

Before Beauregard's victory, troops had been
breaking and running in all directions. General
Bernard Bee had rallied the stricken Southerners
by pointing through the battle smoke and shouting, "There stands Jackson like a stone wall!"

Bee went down under enemy fire, but his troops
rallied. They turned back to fight the Union,
stirred by the sight of "Stonewall" Jackson. The
name stuck, and Jackson became a Southern hero.

But the victory price for First Manassas had
been high. There were 2,000 Southern casualties.
The North lost more. Lee wrote his wife:

> *Do not grieve for the brave dead. Sorrow
> for those who are left behind—friends, rel-
> atives and families. The former are at rest.
> The latter must suffer. The battle will be re-
> peated there in greater force. I hope God will
> again smile on us and strengthen our hearts
> and arms.*

Lee probably heard another story going the
rounds of Richmond after Manassas. Jackson
ordered his men at Manassas to let the Yankees
advance as close as possible before opening fire
and charging with bayonets.

Presbyterian Jackson had said, "When you
charge, yell like Furies." The Rebel Yell, born of
Southern fox hunters' cries, had helped unnerve
the "boys in blue" and turned the tide.

Davis was concerned about the losses in the
western part of the state. He sent Lee, without
authority to act, to see if he could improve the
situation against Union General George B.
McClellan.

With Walter Taylor and Lt. Colonel John A.
Washington as aides, Lee rode into the beautiful
blue hills of Virginia.

"I enjoyed the mountains as I rode along," he
wrote his wife. "The views are magnificent; the
valleys so beautiful and the scenery so peaceful.
What a glorious world Almighty God has given us!
How thankless and ungrateful we are, and how we
labor to mar His gifts."

Lee tried to bring peace to the squabbling
Confederate generals by reasoning with them. He
was a gentleman, soft spoken and polite. An elite
Virginian used to the gentle people who were
taught to be polite, Lee found it hard to "pull rank"
and crack down on the bickering officers.

Lee's great tactician's mind saw that the one-
armed Loring (a veteran of Mexico) should be
attacking the enemy. But, since Loring wouldn't
move, Lee gave in and allowed more troops to be
given to Loring's command, as he wanted.

It was a serious mistake. The other generals took
this as a sign of favoritism to Loring. Other
commanders suspected a weakness in Lee. They
began challenging his orders and strategy. But still
Loring did not move. And Lee had no authority to
force obedience.

To make matters worse, it rained. The ground
was saturated. "I cannot get up sufficient supplies

for the troops to move," Lee explained. It was "quite cool, too. I have on all my winter clothing and am writing in my overcoat," he added.

The rain ruined the gunpowder, dampened the spirits of the men and opened the way for sickness. Taylor wrote, "It is no exaggeration to say that one-half of the army was ineffective." Measles hit hard among the troops.

Lee wrote his wife of another problem common to the field and the civilian areas. "It is so difficult to get our people, unaccustomed to the necessities of war, to comprehend and execute the measures required . . ."

The people simply would not face up to the situation. This was no ninety-day war. It was going to last a long time. And it was going badly for the Virginians in the hills.

Lee was cheered by meeting his son, Rooney. He was now a cavalry major, "cheerful and hearty," as his father wrote, but riding in the rain without his raincoat. Otherwise, there was little to brighten Lee's days in the mountains.

One evening Lee looked up to see a young officer snap a quick salute. "Major Rooney Lee was fired upon by Union pickets, sir, near Cheat Mountain. His companion, Colonel Washington, died instantly. Union pickets put three Minie balls through his body."

Lee's face drained of color.

The soldier's words came quickly. "Your son's mount was shot from under him. Major Lee escaped on Washington's horse, sir." The officer turned.

Lee sighed with relief. The officer faded into the night as grief over Washington's death hit Lee. The boy was the great nephew of the nation's first president. Lee recalled the times he had knelt with

the young officer in private devotions during the
rainy days.

Just about everything was going wrong for Lee.
"Those on the sick list would form an army," he
wrote. They were also difficult to handle. "They
are worse than children, for the latter can be
forced."

The mud grew worse, with reports that mules
died of exertion.

A soldier announced, "Today two mules pulling
a cannon sank so deep in the mud that only their
ears showed." His friends laughed, not knowing
if they could believe him.

Two good things came out of the western
campaign. Lee found a horse he liked to ride. It
was "a Confederate gray," big at sixteen hands
high, and a joy to Lee. But the animal belonged to
another, and so Lee only had the loan of the five-
year-old.

Lee lost his shaving gear when the baggage
wagon got bogged down somewhere. He had a
black mustache a short time before, but his
unshaven face took on a different color. "I have a
beautiful white beard," he wrote to his wife. "It
is much admired."

The troops began calling Lee "Mister Robert," a
kind of familiar title indicating the fondness they
had for him. Soon this became "Marse" Robert, an
even more friendly effort at hominess. It stuck,
and soon Lee was familiarly known by the
distinctly Southern nickname.

The season was growing late in the mountains of
Virginia. Decisive action was difficult before
winter slowed all fighting to a halt. But Lee,
without authority, suggested a strategy to give the
grays a good chance at victory.

After personally scouting the enemy, Lee

planned a surprise attack at Cheat Mountain. The
September 12 assault—the first Lee had planned
in the Civil War—failed because other generals
did not keep their assigned tasks on time.

The element of surprise was lost. It was, in a
sense, Lee's first battle, and he was defeated—not
by the enemy—but by his own officers.

The blow was made worse when Lee dug in for
a defensive action which he knew the North could
not successfully overrun. The union generals,
wisely, also realized this and refused to fight.
Instead, they slipped away.

But Lee said, "The Ruler of the universe . . .
sent a storm to discomfort a well-laid plan, and to
destroy my hopes."

The newspapers back home sent up a howl,
especially when western Virginia withdrew from
Virginia and the South and formed a new state.

Critics in Richmond said Lee should have been
firmer with the officers of the Northwest Army.
But Lee had tried to be the peacemaker—reasoning instead of ordering—with unhappy results.

As October ended, Lee turned back to
Richmond where the newspapers were highly
critical of him. He was pictured, in print, as
"Evacuating Lee" and "Granny Lee." It was
typical of Lee to suffer in silence although Taylor
could see that Lee was bothered by the unfair
articles. The writers didn't know the facts.

Lee even defended his critics to his aide, saying:
"While it was very hard to bear, it was perhaps
quite natural that such hasty conclusions should be
announced." But, Lee added, "It was better not to
attempt a justification of defense, but to go on
steadily in the discharge of duty . . . leaving all
else to the calmer judgment of the future and to
a kind Providence."

Later, Lee mused, "We appointed all our worst generals to command the army and all our best generals to edit the newspapers."

President Davis defended Lee. "He came back, carrying the heavy load of defeat, and unappreciated by the people . . . for they could not know . . . that, if his plans and orders had been carried out, the result would have been victory . . ."

Lee's public image was greatly tarnished, however. In ninety days he had gone from hero to disgrace. Never, in his long military career, had his reputation ever been so low.

Lee turned his mind to his family. This first Christmas away, Lee wrote to his daughter:

I send you some sweet violets that I gathered for you this morning while covered with dense white frost, whose crystals glittered in the bright sun like diamonds, and formed a broach of rare beauty and sweetness which could not be fabricated by the expenditure of a world of money.

The husband was cheerful in a letter to Mary about a sad subject. He wrote near Christmas, "I cannot let this day of grateful rejoicing pass, dear Mary, without some communication with you." He wrote warmly of remembered Christmases with the family at Arlington, which now, he believed, could not be in a "habitable condition" with Union soldiers overrunning it, and "it is better to make up our minds to a general loss."

But if Mary's ancestral home was written off by Lee as lost forever to his family, hope was not gone. "In the absence of a home," he had written, "I wish I could purchase Stratford. That is the only other place I could go to, now accessible to us, that would inspire me with feelings of pleasure and local love."

He continued writing of his boyhood home which he had left for Alexandria before he was old enough for school. "It is a poor place, but we could make enough cornbread and bacon for our support, and the girls could weave us clothes. I wonder if it is for sale and how much. Ask Fitzhugh to try to find out, when he gets to Fredericksburg."

But family matters could not block out the public outcry against Lee which continued.

When President Davis sent Lee to South Carolina to erect defenses, the *Richmond Examiner* said:

He is going where it is hoped he will be far more successful with the spade than with the sword.

Lee went quietly on to his new duties in South Carolina. Sitting in his tent through the cold January days when most military action was frozen in countless harsh positions, Lee based his future on past experiences.

The South, geared for a short war, had already suffered heavily from nearly twenty months of fighting in their own backyard. In spite of tremendous shortages, Lee's Army of Northern Virginia had repeatedly driven back superior Union forces under George McClellan, John Pope and Ambrose E. Burnside. Lincoln had yet to find a general who could outthink Lee. In fact, there were times the North felt as though Lee had looked into their own tents when secret plans were being made. Lee had the uncanny ability to guess what each general would do.

Since the CSA could not win in a long war against superior numbers and supplies, it would be necessary to make the North want peace. The best way to do that, Lee figured, was to bring more pressure on the Federal home front.

Southern victories in the field might force the
North to come to terms.

There were some problems in Lee's plan. He
was commanding general only of the Army of
Northern Virginia, a term he had invented. There
were ten other states in the Confederacy, and he
had no authority over them and no reason to
expect any help from them. They had their own
problems.

Lee was a realist. He had expressed his position
to Mary when rumors had suggested England was
about to enter the war on the side of the South.
"We must make up our minds to fight our own
battles and win our independence alone," Lee
explained. It was still true; he could not count on
help from any place except Virginia.

There were other problems, too, with the need
for speed being top priority. The Virginia soldiers
were "barefoot and poorly clad," and they could
not fight too long in such condition. A quick
victory was necessary if the South was to force the
North to call for peace.

But how was he to achieve a fast, decisive
victory? Five top generals, Lee figured, each
doing a special job, might do what he had in mind.
Thoroughly, carefully, Lee thought through the
strategy he would use if Richmond was attacked.
By the time the spring thaws allowed men and
animals to move across the ground, Lee was ready
for the attack he suspected Lincoln's men would
launch—and which would give Lee his chance for
a quick victory.

Chapter 8

Victory Cheers

Lee, the soldier, stayed clear of political wrangling in South Carolina. While President Davis heard complaints from Beauregard and Johnston, Lee took a short personal trip to visit the burial site of his father, Light Horse Harry Lee, on Cumberland Island off Georgia. Memories of good days rushed before him as he viewed the grave.

In South Carolina, Lee again saw the big gray horse he had so admired in the rainy, dreary days of western Virginia. Major Thomas Broun of the Third Virginia had offered the sixteen-hands-high horse to Lee when they first met, but Lee had declined.

Broun said he had paid $175 for the gray. The horse bred by Andrew Johnston out of Gray Eagle stock, was called Jeff Davis after the Confederate president. It had won first place in county fairs in 1859 and 1860.

Lee had called the horse "my colt" although he had not purchased him in Virginia's hills. Now, in South Carolina, the offer was repeated, except the major wanted the general to have the horse as a gift.

"I can't accept him," Lee explained. "But if you will willingly sell him to me, I will gladly use it for a week or so to learn its qualities."

Lee changed the "Confederate Gray's" name, (as he termed the color) from Jeff Davis to Greenbrier. The general mounted the horse and rode him thirty-five miles that day. Lee paid $200 and took permanent possession of the horse, and again changed the animal's name—from Greenbrier to Traveller.

Lee, a man who had been judging good horseflesh all his life, wrote that the "Confederate Gray" had "fine proportions, strong haunches, flat legs, small head, broad forehead, delicate ears, quick eyes, small feet and a black mane and tail. Such a picture would inspire a poet." Lee and Traveller were together for the duration of the war.

While Lee had been building defenses along the coast, the South had lost Fort Henry in Tennessee to Federal gunboats. Ulysses S. Grant, who had been in Mexico with Lee, grabbed off the Confederacy's Fort Donelson near Fort Henry.

There were other Rebel reverses, too, but the greatest immediate danger was George B. McClellan. His 115,000 Union troops were poised outside Richmond and divided into three units. The red-haired companion of Lee's days in Mexico needed only the spring rains to stop. Then he could strike and take the capital. The nearest armed prong was within seven miles of Richmond.

Lee received word from President Davis on

March 2: "I wish to see you here with the least
delay." Lee hurried to Richmond where bad news
was everywhere.

Defeat was in the air. The people were
preparing to flee. Military records were made
ready for evacuation. Prices of food shot up as
shortages developed. A pound of tea was ten
dollars, an unheard of price; other food items were
equally high. Richmond's people were grim. They
had lost the singing, flag-waving attitude of a few
months before.

Through these silent, numbed citizens Lee
made his way to the inner circles of official
Richmond. There Lee was told "Richmond will be
abandoned."

Lee was not often known to show emotion. But
this news distressed him. His voice revealed his
deep feelings. "Richmond must not be given up; it
shall not be given up," he exclaimed.

Lee explained his position in a letter to his wife.
"It will give me great pleasure to do everything I
can to relieve him [Davis] and serve the country,
but I do not see either advantage or pleasure to my
duties."

Lee was hampered by technicalities of
command. Jeff Davis saw himself as a soldier. He
had made Lee a public figure of command while
keeping control himself. Davis was fighting with
Congress, and Lee was limited in what he could do
for Virginia. So, as official commanding general
but "under the direction of the President" and
without authority, Lee planned the relief of
Richmond. He had to work around the difficulty.

Lee reasoned that defending Richmond was not
wise. Instead he believed attacking the poised
McClellan armies would be a surprise and might
force the Union troops back to Washington.
McClellan had divided his troops into three

attacking groups. But how does a smaller force defeat three Union armies?

With boldness, Lee decided. If he could strike hard enough at one Union unit, the surprise and swiftness might confuse the other two. But such a daring plan needed unusually brave leaders who would obey orders.

Lee wanted Stonewall Jackson to strike Union generals Milroy, Banks and McDowell. Union troops were near Fredericksburg. When hit hard by Confederates, President Lincoln might fear the Rebels were striking for Washington, a few miles away. This was psychological warfare—Lee knew how much fear played in battles.

There was one problem: Jackson was technically under command of Joe Johnston, not Lee. Johnston was sensitive, unhappy with Lee and Davis. Still, Lee knew he needed the dependable Jackson to pull off part of the plan to relieve Richmond.

In the May 31 battle near Richmond known as Four Oaks to the North and Seven Pines to the South, Johnston was severely wounded. Lee and Davis, under fire at the scene, saw Johnston carried by on a litter. He had a ball in his shoulder and a shell loaded with musket balls near his spine.

The president dismounted as the general was loaded onto an ambulance wagon. Johnston opened his eyes, smiled and gave Davis his hand.

The president and Virginia's official but powerless commanding general rode back to Richmond that night. Davis twisted in his saddle and spoke to Lee, giving him command. It was that casual.

Suddenly, without warning, Lee was in charge of a half fought battle. With his plans already thought out, Lee moved to execute his surprise tactic on McClellan.

He called in Jackson and explained a bold
strategy. It required swift movement by the major
general. Lee's plan was a master stroke if properly
executed, and the tall, silent Presbyterian layman
was the one Lee thought could do it. Jackson was
one general who would rather fight the enemy
than his peers. And Jackson could not only take
orders; he could carry them out.

This was true of another man called in to help
the Richmond plan. Jeb Stuart, frankly
disappointed that Lee had been named
commander, still obeyed Lee. Stuart, as one of the
South's more dashing horsemen, had circled 150
miles around the enemy position, returning with
valuable intelligence information.

With Lee's daring plan and Jackson's swift
action, three Northern generals soon reeled back
in confusion and pain. Moving fast, Jackson hit
Milroy and defeated him. Then Jackson spun
around and surprised Banks. This second Union
unit stood up to fight, but wilted under Jackson's
slashing offensive. Soon Bank's troopers were
driven across the Potomac.

There remained one more Union threat. This
one, Lee had figured, was to be fought primarily
as a war of nerves. Would McDowell link up with
McClellan and strike Richmond as one unit, or
would McDowell become fearful and retreat?

On May 27, word came that McDowell was
moving south, apparently to link up with the red-
haired McClellan. But, two days later the report
changed.

"Sir, he must believe he is facing superior
forces," an officer said. "McDowell has turned
back!" A slight smile slipped across Lee's face as
he heard the report. His strategy had triumphed.

Fearing for his own safety and that of

Washington, McDowell followed fellow officers Milroy and Banks north. General Stonewall Jackson, following Lee's tactics, had done the impossible!

The combination of sudden high morale on the South's part and fear on the North's with Jackson's victories sent McClellan fleeing. His routed troops strewed equipment all along the line of retreat. By the end of June, the man who had almost touched Richmond was told by President Lincoln to "save your army at all events."

McClellan, surprised that Lee had attacked his superior forces, had learned too late that Lee was a superior strategist. Within ninety days of Lee's return to Richmond, the two hostile army's positions were completely reversed.

Now Lincoln feared Washington was in danger. Lee reasoned that the North might sue for peace if the pressure was kept up.

More Southern victories followed that summer. Lee's new Army of Northern Virginia won at Cedar Run (Slaughter's Mountain) and Second Manassas. Confederate troops were now at Washington's door.

But Lee did not attack. His men were tired and hungry. They could not live off the land because it had already been scoured clean. The Confederate's supply lines were stretched so thin that there was not enough food or ammunition. Lee reasoned that it was a military necessity to stop short of Washington, which was heavily defended with fresh troops.

Leaders in the Confederacy knew the South's condition was somewhat relieved after Union General John Pope's defeat at Second Manassas. The North took one of the worst beatings of the war. The braggart Pope, whom Lincoln had sent

to replace McClellan, fled in such disarray that he
left great quantities of Union supplies for the
ragged, hungry Rebels.

After the summer's victories, Lee expressed his
gratitude to God. Slowly he penned a general
order to the troops:

> *The commanding general, profoundly
> grateful to the Giver of all victory for the
> signal success which He has blessed our arms,
> tenders his warmest thanks and congratula-
> tions to the army, by whose valor such splen-
> did results have been achieved.*

By September, Lee's need for supplies had
become so critical that he had to seek food in
another source: the North. Lee decided to invade
Maryland.

On September 5, some 55,000 Rebels began
crossing the Potomac. The invaders had been
invaded. Lincoln was forced to put McClellan
back in command, replacing Pope. This time he
would be more respectful of Lee's brilliant
military mind.

The Rebels did not make a pretty sight,
marching into Maryland. But they were in high
spirits, some singing as they marched.

A Northern eyewitness said, "They were dirty,
lank, ugly specimens of humanity, with shocks of
hair sticking through the holes in their hats, and the
dust thick on their dirty faces, these men who had
driven back—again and again—our splendid
legions."

Lee hoped his invasion would cause the Union
garrison to pull out of Harper's Ferry. When this
didn't happen, Lee assigned Jackson to seize the
arsenal to protect the rear of Lee's tattered
soldiers.

The next part of Lee's plan could have been put
into effect if it had not been for a strange incident.

One of Lee's officers lost a package of cigars containing Lee's strategy. The information was found by a Union soldier and forwarded to McClellan. Now he had a distinct advantage: he knew as much about Lee's plans as Lee himself.

McClellan, usually a slow, cautious fighter, confident because he had Lee's battle plans, moved boldly toward Sharpsburg.

On September 14, Lee was ready to abandon the Maryland invasion and return to Virginia, but changed his mind when Jackson sent word he had taken Harper's Ferry with 13,000 arms. With hundreds of Union wagons also seized, the South was in a position to continue—but ran into the 87,000 McClellan forces at Sharpsburg.

Lee's 41,000 troops, in poor physical condition and short of everything, clashed with the well-equipped Union forces in a long, bloody battle.

Union fire was so heavy that every stalk of corn in one field "was cut as closely as could have been done with a knife."

"We had hidden in the field at dawn," a wounded Rebel soldier told the doctor. "A mist and the standing corn protected us. But the sun drove the mist away, and cannister stripped the corn. Almost every man died in rows where we had hidden from the unexpected attack." The doctor shook his weary head as stretcher after stretcher of hopeless cases came into the field hospital.

No battle ever fought on the North American continent spilled more blood in a single day. About 10,700 Southern casualties were counted. McClellan lost a little over 12,400 men. The North called the battle Antietam and the South called it Sharpsburg.

If McClellan had followed up his advantage, there is doubt the South could have survived. But

Lee, often credited with uncanny ability to think exactly what his opponents were planning, reasoned that the firey-haired Union officer would not fight the next day.

As usual, Lee was right. After midnight, Lee escaped. He led the way back across the Potomac in the chilly dawn. The Maryland invasion was over by September 19.

Lee returned to Virginia and more bad news.

Taylor, Lee's long-time aide and now a major, entered the tent which Lee always insisted upon using as long as his troops had to sleep in the field. The general was looking over papers, reading from the stack of morning mail. Taylor left the tent and then came back.

"With my accustomed freedom," Taylor said he entered the headquarters tent without announcement. "I was startled and shocked to see him overcome with grief, an open letter in his hands."

The letter carried the sad news the Lee's twenty-three-year-old daughter, Ann Carter Lee, had died of a swift, terrible fever.

Lee wrote his wife, "I cannot express the anguish I feel at the death of our sweet Annie. To know that I shall never see her again on earth, that her place in our circle, which I always hoped one day to enjoy, is forever vacant, is agonizing in the extreme."

"But God," he concluded the letter, "in this, as in all things, has mingled mercy with the blow, in selecting that one best prepared to leave us. May you be able to join me in saying, 'His will be done.' "

The North did not like the turn of the war.

McClellan, Lincoln said, should have pursued Lee after Antietam instead of allowing him to escape. He again replaced McClellan, putting General Ambrose E. Burnside in against Lee.

Burnside, on December 13, tried to dislodge Confederates at Fredericksburg. More than 12,600 Union soldiers fell to somewhat more than 5,000 Confederates.

"Our losses are so heavy it's nothing less than a massacre," moaned a Union soldier. Blood ran across his face from a scalp wound. "Every officer in sight has been mowed down."

In the battle, Lee looked down from a hill at the carnage below and said to Longstreet, "It is well that war is so terrible; we should grow too fond of it."

As 1862 slid to a bloody close, Lee recalled the battle which had defeated Burnside. The Army of Northern Virginia was cited for "high appreciation of the fortitude, valor and devotion displayed by them, which, under the blessing of Almighty God, have added the victory of Fredericksburg to their long list of triumphs."

Lee was pleased with his troops, but Lee's gratitude was "to Him who hath given us the victory."

Lee observed his second Christmas by inviting some officers into his tent. "Perhaps you gentlemen would like something to drink," he said. There was a teasing light in his eyes and a hint of a joke, for he knew some of them liked a little glass of spirits now and then. Several officers knew a demijohn had been brought to the tent of their non-drinking commander. Tin cups were handed to the men who lifted the expected drink to their lips and tasted—buttermilk!

His 1862 Christmas letter to Mary was tinged with philosophy. "What a cruel thing is war. To separate families . . . and friends, and to mar the purest joys and happiness God has granted us in this world."

Lee spoke of war as filling hearts with hatred instead of love. He added, "I pray that on this day when 'peace and good will' are preached to all mankind, that better thoughts will fill the hearts of our enemies and turn them to peace."

For Lee, 1862 had been as gloriously successful as 1861 had been bad. He knew the secret of peace in his own life. Others marveled at this quality in him. But where was "peace and good will" for the country as 1863 approached?

Chapter 9

Five Confederate Generals

Five Virginia generals were carefully chosen for Lee's 1863 campaigns. There was the dependable, serious-minded Stonewall Jackson. There was also Jeb Stuart, another fighting man of strong religious convictions.

James Longstreet, senior division commander, was familiarly called "Ole Pete." He had one major flaw as a fighter: he was slow in action. However, Lee had to take a chance because Longstreet was a fine, all-around soldier.

Richard H. Anderson and A.P. Hill rounded out Lee's top five most-proven generals. These two needed more experience. But Lee thought they were qualified for the campaigns he planned.

Lincoln also worked on improving the Union's

command. Burnside was replaced by Joseph Hooker.

Lee wrote of a new problem on March 27. "I have felt so unwell." He had not been able to go anywhere and was suffering from a heavy cold. The doctors ordered him out of the tent and into a private home near Fredericksburg where he could have a bed. Further examination followed Lee's symptoms of a "good deal of pain in my chest, back and arms. It came on in paroxysms." The doctors called it "an inflammation of the heartsac." Modern doctors believe Lee had suffered a mild heart attack with permanent damage to his heart.

Sandy-haired Joe Hooker was moving by the middle of April, and Lee, who was "feeble and worthless and can do but little" as he wrote Mary, had to move his 60,000 ill-equipped troops against Hooker's 130,000 well-provisioned blue-clad soldiers. The two-to-one disadvantage was tested at Chancellorsville.

As usual, Lee seemed to know what his opponent would do. He called in Jackson and explained he thought the Federals would attack with General John Sedgwick backing Hooker. Lee ordered troops at Fredericksburg to watch Sedgwick while he concentrated on Hooker.

Jackson, wearing a full dark beard, sat on a cracker box while his commander, similarly seated, finished telling his plans. But Lee was one to let his generals speak before ordering them to action.

"General Jackson," Lee said, "what do you propose to do?"

Jackson referred to the map. Chancellorsville had only one mansion and some small buildings in a wilderness clearing. But now 50,000 unwelcome Federal visitors were camped there.

Jackson pointed a long finger. He traced a route through the woods shown on the map. "Go through there," Jackson said.

"What troops will you need?"

"My whole corps," Jackson's hand stroked his bearded chin.

Lee was thoughtful. Jackson's 28,000 men would try to sweep around the vastly superior forces. Lee would be left with about 15,000 men, for Anderson was using troops to build breastworks and the other Virginia generals had more soldiers.

Lee decided to let Jackson make the sweep. Stonewall moved off while Lee waited.

At shortly after five o'clock that afternoon, Jackson's corps followed a bugle corps to action. They caught the blue-clad soldiers cooking dinner, unaware of danger at their backs.

These particular soldiers were mostly Germans, paid to fight for the North. They didn't speak much, if any, English. Their surprise turned to terror. They ran. Jackson's boldness had triumphed again!

In all the war, no sweep had been more successful. But there was a terrible price. Lee learned about it in the deep three o'clock darkness the next morning.

"Stonewall Jackson has been severely wounded," reported Captain Wilbourn, Jackson's signal officer.

Lee sat up. "What?"

"It was an accident; his own men. It's serious."

Lee cried, "Ah, Captain! Any victory is dearly bought which deprives us of General Jackson, even for a short time."

Wilbourn said he had been riding with Jackson in the darkness after the surprised Federal troops were routed. Confederate shots had rung out sharply, striking Jackson in the right hand and left arm. The wound had come from his own men. "The surgeons are trying to save the arm," Wilbourn added.

Lee got up from the ground where he had been laying under a waterproof cloth. He sent Jackson a note:

> Could I have directed events, I would have chosen for the good of the country to be disabled in your stead. I congratulate you upon the victory, which is due to your skill and energy.

The battle continued into the morning. Lee was observed, unruffled on Traveller's back, as shells burst around him and shot plowed up the ground.

The wounded were trying to crawl from the places where flames still flared in the brush. The soldier's faces were blackened with battle.

Lee guided the big gray horse toward the Chancellorsville mansion which was burning as Hooker retreated and the tide of battle passed. The weary Virginians, seeing Lee, gave a mighty Rebel yell. It was their way of honoring the gray-bearded man who had again given the Army of Northern Virginia a victory against superior odds.

The yell of praise was mixed with screams of the dying and wounded. There were 13,000 Southern casualties at Chancellorsville, but the Union had lost 17,000 men. A report came that Jackson's arm had to be amputated. Lee knew that infection was now the big danger. He sent another message: "He has lost his left arm, but I have lost my right arm."

Chancellorsville had been a Southern victory, but at terrible price.

While waiting for further details on Jackson, Lee surveyed the military situation. Through a mixup in orders, Sedgwick had been allowed to move from Fredericksburg. It posed the possibility he would link up with Hooker, who had fled across the Rappahannock River.

On May 6 word came that Jackson had developed pneumonia. Lee, recalling that he and Jackson had attended religious services together on April 26, sent another note of encouragement to the sinking Jackson. "Give him my affectionate regards, and tell him to make haste and get well."

Lee knelt and prayed in the destruction which had been Chancellorsville. He prayed with agony of spirit while his troops slept and Jackson fought for life.

Lee went to church services on Sunday. A chaplain told Lee that Stonewall was slipping fast toward death. Lee shook his head, remembering that Jackson had expressed a wish to die on the Sabbath.

Lee cried, "Surely General Jackson must recover! God will not take him from us, now that we need him so much. Surely he will be spared to us, in answer to the many prayers which are offered for him."

When the services were over, Lee approached the chaplain with another message for Jackson. "When you return, I trust you will find him better . . . give him my love, and tell him that I wrestled in prayer for him last night, as I never prayed, I believe, for myself."

Lee turned sharply away, as the chaplain guessed, so the clergyman would not see the deep emotion the general felt.

He was in his headquarters tent some time later when he heard a whispered conversation outside. Lee raised his head expectantly. The dark eyes, now alert with questioning hope, saw a paper in the soldier's hands.

Lee took it quickly. The awful truth crept over

him like a chill. Jackson's mind had wandered far in the coma which pneumonia brought. He had talked much, saying military things. Then Jackson said, quite clearly, but in a low voice: "Let us pass over the river, and rest under the shade of the trees."

With those words, he died.

Lee had indeed lost his right arm; he lost one of his only aggressive, fighting generals who would follow orders.

The loss of "the great and good Jackson" caused Lee to weep. But there was little time to mourn. If Lee was still to force the North to come to terms, he had to keep moving. An invasion of Pennsylvania was designed to bring more pressure on the Northern home front and make the people there seek peace.

Soon fresh field crops would be ripe in Pennsylvania, where the war had not touched. Peas and beans would be available for Lee's hungry men. Once his objectives there were met, he could move on toward Northern cities.

Lee's second invasion of the North pulled pursuit by Hooker's replacement, George Meade. Lincoln was still trying to find one general who could compete with the Virginian who always seemed to know Union officers' plans.

It was also Lee's hope that Ulysses S. Grant would be concerned about the Pennsylvania invasion and relieve his battering assaults on Vicksburg, a city which controlled traffic on the Mississippi River.

Gettysburg was a small Pennsylvania village in the path of Lee's army. In early July the gray troopers marched toward it.

Union dismounted cavalrymen with new, eight-shot Spencer repeating carbines happened to be in the crossroads town. The blues and grays clashed in an unplanned battle. And the Rebels' manpower drove the Federals back in spite of their superior firepower.

Survivors of the unexpected first firing dug in along Cemetery Hill south of town, giving the North an advantage. Lee ordered Richard Ewell to attack this position. But Ewell delayed while reinforcements came up. This cost Lee his first major chance for victory. The Northern trenches grew deeper in the delay.

Longstreet of the First Corps was always a slow, cautious fighter. He tried to talk Lee into waiting for the Federals to attack while the Confederates dug into a strong position.

Lee was fighting blind, lacking reports from cavalry scouts under Stuart. Lee said, "In the absence of reports from him, I am in ignorance as to what we have in front of us here. It may be the whole Federal army; it may be only a detachment."

The situation grew worse when Longstreet delayed going into action as ordered by Lee. On July 2 Ewell was late in attacking because he was waiting for the sound of Longstreet's guns before moving.

The battle raged into the third day without a Confederate victory. "Lee is not feeling well," a soldier said.

"He walks as if he is weak and in pain," a cavalryman remarked.

But the fight had not gone out of the general. He met with Longstreet in the early morning, pointed at a map and said, "The enemy is there, and I am going to strike him there."

Close to 12,000 brave young men from many Confederate states made up Pickett's Charge. They swept forward along Cemetery Ridge where 6,000 Federals popped up from behind

fences, trees and stone walls. Thousands of Confederates dropped from a hail of lead. Some reached the stone walls and vaulted them.

But it was hopeless, Lee saw from his seat on Traveller's broad back. The general urged the big gray toward the men who were fleeing in panic. He was engaged in "rallying and in encouraging the broken troops, and was riding about a little in front of the wood, quite alone," an observer said. Lee called to the bloody, walking wounded, urging them to take up a musket and fight again.

The British observer said, "I saw many badly wounded men take off their hats and cheer him." They picked up weapons and went back to fight again and some to die.

Lee rode up to the visiting military officer. "This has been a sad day, Colonel," Lee said, "a sad day." The general suggested shelter for the visitor because shells were bursting all around.

When another general emotionally tried to tell Lee what had happened, Lee replied, "Never mind, General; all this has been my fault. It is I that have lost this fight, and you must help me out of it the best way you can."

In the aftermath of battle, Lee came upon a wounded Union soldier on the ground. The bluecoat looked up at Lee on his big gray horse and cried, "Hurrah for the Union!"

Lee dismounted and walked slowly toward the fallen man. The soldier thought Lee was personally going to kill him.

The general stuck out his right hand. "My son," he said gently, "I hope you will soon be well."

Lee was taking the blame for the losses of July 3, but the South had won the day before.

Colonel C.S. Veneble of Lee's staff said he had

heard Lee order Longstreet to send in extra
support divisions, which was not done.

"I know," Lee answered, "I know."

In the six weeks since Jackson had died, Lee had
found that he had indeed lost his right hand. Other
generals did not obey, or delayed action as a form
of disobedience. And Lee, never schooled in
dealing harshly with men of high station, showed
again this weakness.

It was after midnight when Lee finally returned
to his tent. The big gray horse was tired, and Lee
was unwell and exhausted. The general had to be
helped out of the saddle.

A cavalryman watched Lee as he leaned heavily
against the horse's solid flank. The moon shone on
the general's face. It had "an expression of sadness
that I had never before seen upon his face."

Lee surveyed the price of Gettysburg. He sent a
message to Richmond by a cavalry general with
the results.

Actually, the Union had lost three thousand
more men than the Confederacy. But the North
could stand the loss; the South could not.

Lee ordered a retreat from Pennsylvania.

The turning point of the war had been reached.

On July 4, 1863, Lee headed for Richmond in
heavy rain. But more bad news awaited him there.

On the same day, Lee learned Grant pounded
Vicksburg, Mississippi, into submission. The
determined Grant had chopped the Western
Confederates from their partners; the Union now
controlled the Mississippi River. Grant, as
Lincoln's only winning general, would be free for
other assignments.

In Richmond, President Davis was
understanding of Lee's Pennsylvania failure, but
as usual the press was not. The criticism grew so

severe over the next several weeks that Lee offered his resignation.

Davis was wiser than the press. "Our country could not afford to lose you," he assured Lee. "Where am I to find that new commander who is to possess the greater ability which you believe to be required?" the president asked. He returned Lee to duty, his rank unchanged.

Lee got personal bad news before 1863 was over. His son, Rooney, had been captured by Federal cavalry units as he was recuperating from a wound. Rooney's wife, Charlotte (who had earlier lost a son, Lee's grandson) was greatly shaken by the experience. On Christmas Day, Lee got more sad news: Charlotte, his only daughter-in-law, had died.

Lee sat in his tent that Christmas of 1863 and remembered the good things of the past, including his favorite lemon cake, and his children laughing about the table. Hopefully, 1864 would be more pleasant, but there were serious problems which Lee knew no mortal alone could overcome.

Chapter 10

Gray Line Grows Thin

Shortages were beginning to hurt the entire South. Needs were especially painful in the Army of Northern Virginia as 1864 began.

"Provisions for the men, too, are very scarce," Lee wrote Mary after noting there was no forage for the horses. The soldiers, not the army, owned the animals they rode. There was little money for guns and none for hay—even if it had been available.

Some soldiers had been without shoes the previous winter. Now it was worse. One division reported that more than four hundred men were barefoot. More than a thousand were without blankets.

Lee wrote, "With very light diet and light clothing, I fear they will suffer. But still they are cheerful and uncomplaining."

The Virginia soldiers prepared huts for themselves of whatever they could find, or spent the winter in ragged tents now showing signs of a long, hard war.

Things were not going well, especially in Tennessee where Longstreet had been sent against Grant. Lincoln's only winning general had racked up victories at Chicamauga and Chattanooga.

If there was nothing but bad news from the military standpoint in early 1864, Lee had reason to feel better about the spiritual condition of his troops. Revival was sweeping the ranks.

The Rev. B.T. Lacey, who had been Stonewall Jackson's chaplain, came with Chaplain J. William Jones to see Lee. Lee greeted them that February 6 and listened to their report.

"A great revival has extended through the camps and is bringing thousands of our noble men to Christ," Jones reported.

Chaplain Jones saw Lee's dark eyes brighten and "his whole countenance glow with pleasure." The chaplain felt the whole tent was warmed by Lee's favorable response.

The next day, Lee issued a general order. Noting he had already called for proper observance of the Sabbath, the commanding general was now repeating "the order on the subject."

Lee was pleased that many brigades had erected "convenient houses of worship," but he ordered all duties stopped on the Sabbath for men and animals, except where absolutely necessary.

On the military front, shortage of provisions and news of a new Union general for the Army of the Potomac made Lee thoughtful. In January, Lee wrote the secretary of war that "a regular supply of provisions to the troops in this army is a matter of great importance."

When they were hungry, the men suffered morale loss. Desertions were "becoming more frequent." Lee added, "Unless there is a change, I fear the army cannot be kept together."

The Northern newspapers carried stories that Lincoln had finally found a Union officer who would win in the field. Lincoln personally made Grant a lieutenant general with authority over *all* Union troops everywhere. Lee was still only in charge of Virginia's forces.

By March 25, Lee had guessed Grant's intentions. "I now know that the first important effort will be directed against Richmond," Lee wrote Davis. Lee knew Grant and had seen him operate in Mexico.

Lee quickly figured that Grant would take action against Longstreet, now in the west. "It behooves us to be on the alert," Lee wrote Longstreet, "or we will be deceived. You know that is part of Grant's tactics."

Longstreet, slow to fight, was also slow to understand the military skills of Lincoln's new general. "I do not think that he is any better than Pope," Longstreet told Lee in April. "His chief strength is in his prestige."

Lee knew better. In a conversation with a colonel, Lee said Grant and Meade would be a tough combination. Yet Lee was not discouraged.

"Colonel, we have to whip them. We must whip them, and it has already made me feel better to think of it." Lee flashed a smile.

The winter snows were gone from the fields. Signs of spring meant the beginning of another hard season of battles.

Grant and Lee clashed first at the Wilderness Campaign. Lee had upward of 65,000 men, Grant was believed to have 100,000 troops. The Union leader was west of Fredericksburg slicing south to cut the heart out of the Confederacy at Richmond.

Always an offensive fighter who carried the battle to the enemy, Lee struck first. In the battle of May 5-7, wounded and dead soon sprawled in horrible mounds. Near-by plantation mansions became bloody, smelly hospitals where men moaned and died.

A Union trooper, storming through the wilderness, wrote of the untended wounded and ungathered dead. They lay, he recorded, "thick in the jungle of scrub oaks, pines and underbrush, through which we rushed upon them."

The area caught fire, and flames raced through the brush with such intensity and speed that neither North nor South could help the man who could not move out of the inferno on his own.

Grant's counterattack against Lee's initial onslaught was blunted. Lee's Confederates defeated the Union left flank, turned back the center and slowed the right. Union generals Burnside and Hooker retreated under a devastating pounding. But Grant was made of sterner stuff.

He pulled back from the Wilderness where the dry vines, trees and shrubs still burned. The air was hideous with the cries of trapped, wounded and dying men of both sides. But Grant was not retreating.

He slipped off to the east, a little closer to Fredericksburg, but then turned south again toward Richmond, skirting Lee's forces.

Lee's uncanny ability to predict his opposing general's next move prompted Lee to place Confederate troops at Spotsylvania where he figured Grant would reappear.

Lee waited, knowing he was finally up against a

determined, tough-minded Union officer who
wanted to win; the price was not as important as
victory.

Lee had now lost the services of Longstreet. As
usual, Longstreet had been slow in coming up with
his troops at the Wilderness. His men begun
calling this tendency "the slows."

But he would not fight again for a long time. A
shot fired by his own men hit Longstreet high in
the chest at the throat. It seemed to be a fatal
wound, but Longstreet lived.

Two of Lee's top five generals were out of
action: Jackson dead, Longstreet badly wounded.
The third fell on May 12.

Word came to Lee that his dashing cavalry
officer, Jeb Stuart, had been wounded in the
stomach as he faced Philip Sheridan at Yellow
Tavern. A short time later an officer entered Lee's
tent and told him Stuart was dead.

"I can scarcely think of him without weeping,"
Lee said when the officer came upon the general a
few minutes later.

He wrote Mary that, "a more zealous, ardent,
brave and devoted soldier than Stuart the
Confederacy cannot have. Praise be to God for
having sustained him to us so far."

Lee himself barely escaped death in the bitter
fighting. Grant, the hammerer, threw his assault
troops on the Confederates' prepared breastworks known first as the Mule Shoe and later as
Bloody Angle.

The South's fortifications were shaped like a
"U" or a "V," with the open end to the south. Grant
had determined "to fight it out on this line if it
takes all summer." He wanted his men to take the
great mounds of dirt.

On the day Stuart died, "the most remarkable

musketry fire of the war" pounded the earthworks. Taylor, on Lee's personal staff, recorded that the lines released such "hissing fire" that there was "an incessant, terrific hail of deadly missiles."

It was so bad that "no living man nor thing could stand in the doomed space embraced within those angry lines; even large trees were felled—their trunks cut in twain by the bullets of small arms."

The Spotsylvania battle lasted twelve terrible days. Death repeatedly reached out for General Lee, but never quite touched him.

The usually-steady Traveller suddenly reared as heavy artillery fire opened in front of him. He reared just as a solid shot passed under his belly, missing Lee's boot heel and imbedding in the ground. God had spared Lee again.

Lee was riding forward when he found his men running in great disorder. He raised himself in the stirrups and called to them.

"Shame on you, men! Shame on you! Go back to your regiments!"

The men continued their headlong flight, panicked out of all reason by the fury of the Union fire. Lee moved toward the battle they were leaving in such fear.

General Gordon, riding with Lee, saw that the general "rode majestically in front of my line of battle." Lee's head was uncovered and "he looked a very god of war."

Realizing that Lee intended to lead the men back into battle, Gordon spurred his mount up beside the big gray. "General Lee," Gordon said firmly but so low the soldiers could not hear, "you shall not lead my men in a charge! No man can do that, sir!"

Gordon gently blocked Traveller with his own

horse while explaining to Lee that there were Carolinians and Virginians in the gray ranks behind.

"They have never failed you on any field," Gordon said with feeling, "and they will not fail you here." His voice had risen; the men overheard. "No!" the men cried, "No!" They had not failed Marse Robert; they would not fail him now.

Gordon was firm. "General Lee, this is no place for you. Go back, General; we will drive them back!"

Soldiers gathered around Lee. Some turned Traveller with his bridle. Then, hanging on to bridle and stirrups, some pushing against the horse, the men seemed literally to be pulling their general to safety.

Gently, Lee brought the big gray's head back toward the enemy. The other men cheered, but those closest to Lee again grabbed the bridle and tried to turn the horse toward safety. An attack commenced, spilling lead all around them. The men intensified their cries for Lee to go back.

"If you will promise to drive those people from our works," Lee said gently, "I will go back." They kept their word after Lee moved back.

Another time, disorganized troops fell back where Lee sat on Traveller. He called to General McGowan, "Is this splendid brigade of yours running like a flock of geese?"

General McGowan assured Lee the men were not whipped. "They only want a place to form, and they will fight as well as ever they did."

Minie balls whizzed around Lee. He saw three Texas regiments moving forward across deadly, open ground. Lee turned Traveller around and waved his hat. "Hurrah for Texas! Hurrah for Texas!"

As the newcomers rushed by, acknowledging

their general's tribute, he called after them to give
the Union "the cold steel." He shouted, "They will
stand and fire all day and never move unless you
charge them."

A soldier recorded, "Never before in my
life . . . did I ever witness such a scene as was
enacted when Lee pronounced those words. A yell
rent the air that must have been heard for miles
around."

Tears slid down the cheeks of a veteran courier
at the scene. He exclaimed, "I would charge hell
itself for that old man!"

The general tried to move toward the battle, but
the Texans cried that they would not advance until
Lee turned back. Colonel Veneble, Lee's aide,
moved up beside Lee and pointed out that
reinforcements had come up.

Lee turned Traveller's head away from the
battle. The cheering Texans moved on to fight.
They made the Union soldiers in the underbrush
aware of their power by inflicting heavy
casualties. Grant's troops reeled and fell back
under the Rebel attack.

The inspired Rebels wrested another victory
from the Union. But it was not the kind of triumph
the South needed, for Grant again slipped away;
but not in retreat. He had set his eyes on
Richmond, and nothing could shake him from that
goal except death—his own death.

Lee, who knew this opponent as he did his
previous ones, said that Grant had an iron will. Lee
realized Grant was a persistent man who would
continue to deliver "constant and heavy blows."

Furthermore, Lee explained, Grant was in so
solidly with the Union government that he could
"command to any extent its limitless resources in
men and materials, while the confederacy was
already practically exhausted in both."

Lee predicted, however, that the Union could not long continue the heavy losses they were sustaining.

Lee was right. When Grant had suffered an incredible 60,000 casualties, he broke off the direct attack on Richmond. He skirted east and drove south toward Cold Harbor.

Lee kept his thinning forces between Grant and Richmond, clashing again on June 3. The Union lost another 7,000 men, causing Grant to give up his tactic of sending waves of blue-clad soldiers across open ground against dug-in Confederates.

Grant moved southeast of the capital, swinging into a new phase of the war against Petersburg. If Grant took the city of 18,000 people, he would be within twenty-five miles of Richmond—this time to the south of it.

Lee had no time for rejoicing. He was still in poor health and short three top generals, plus several other high officers. Still, he had held Grant's 100,000 bluecoats from taking Richmond from the north and east. Lee had done that with about 45,000 men.

On June 17, Beauregard's small force at Petersburg was in trouble. He warned Lee that "unless reinforcements are sent within forty-eight hours, God Almighty alone can save Petersburg."

Lee arrived with troops the next morning, and set up his tent.

Petersburg was temporarily safe. But, as he left Cold Harbor, Lee had predicted what would happen if Grant crossed the James River: "It will become a siege, and then it will be a mere question of time."

Chapter 11

Moaning in the Wind

Lee did not know that Grant agreed with him. Grant wrote, "it was a mere question of arithmetic to calculate how long they [the Confederates] could hold out." He expected to win the war with his next campaign.

The people at home—North and South—were tired of the war. Losses had been heavy on both sides. The Union had replacements and could afford the casualties. The Confederates could not. Time, too, was on Grant's side. The South's supplies were running out.

Lee, looking out over the siege trenches Grant had dug around Petersburg, reported to President Davis: "I think it is his [Grant's] purpose to compel the evacuation of our present situation by cutting off supplies." Grant would not have to use military arms; starvation would do his work for him.

Shells continued to fall in Petersburg. The community, sitting on the banks of the Appomattox River, had been a place of sturdy brick houses and stately magnolia trees. Now it

was a torn, starving city. It was ringed by twenty-
six miles of earthen breastworks. These mounds
gave the Union troops safety from Lee's thinly
spread defenders.

Lee was now busy protecting Richmond from
two sides. The Federals had Spencer repeating
rifles. Lee's troops were down to picking up spent
musket balls to remelt and shoot again. Lack of
food, especially fresh fruits and vegetable, caused
scurvy to rage among Lee's weakened troops. The
disease brought on bleeding gums and bleeding
under the skin. Milk went to two dollars a quart
in Petersburg, if it could be found.

Inflation and scarcity had also hurt Richmond.
In December, J.B. Jones wrote in his diary, that
"there is deep vexation in the city . . . our affairs
are rapidly approaching a crisis." He "saw selling
at auction today second-hand shirts at forty-
dollars each and blankets at seventy-five."

In early February 1865 President Davis, under
heavy criticism for the many losses, was forced to
do what many believe he should have done at the
beginning of the war. Congress approved, and
Lee was named general-in-chief of all
Confederate armies. Now he was equal to Grant in
authority.

Lee's faith showed in the statement he issued
accepting the new post. "Deeply impressed with
the difficulties and responsibilities of the position,
and humbly invoking the guidance of almighty
God, I rely for success upon the courage and
fortitude of the army, sustained by the patriotism
and firmness of the people, confident that their
united efforts under the blessing of heaven will
secure peace and independence."

But it was too late. "Unless the men and animals
can be subsisted," Lee reported early in March,

"the army cannot be kept together, and our present lines must be abandoned."

Lee went to Richmond and reported personally to Congress. He had little food. Very thin lines stretched almost to the breaking point. And the 1865 spring campaigns had not yet begun.

While he was near the capital, some firing broke out. Unconcerned about his own personal safety, Lee walked near the firing toward something which had attracted his attention. Witnesses saw the general stoop and pick up a young sparrow. He returned it to the nest and went back to his horse as the battle continued.

There was moaning in the wind; suffering and sorrow touched everyone. The end was in sight. Desertions climbed sharply as families sent word to sons and husbands in the Confederate lines of starvation and death at home. Torn between duty at home and on the battlefront, many soldiers chose home.

The war-weary soldiers were thinking of what the conflict was all about. One of Lee's young lieutenants wrote lines which expressed how many on both sides were feeling after four years of war:

As we lay there watching the bright stars, many a soldier asked himself, "What is all this about?" Why is it that two hundred thousand men of one blood and tongue, believing in the fatherhood of God and the universal brotherhood of man, should, in the nineteenth century of the Christian Era, be thus armed with all the improved appliances of modern warfare, and seeking one another's lives?

The lieutenant added a wistful sentence: "We could settle our differences by compromising and all be home in ten days."

Lee had noted in a year-end letter to Mary, "I pray daily, and almost hourly, to our heavenly Father to come to the relief of you and our afflicted country. I know He will order all things for our good, and we must be content."

The horrible war dragged on into spring, when the muddy ground would soon permit movements of massive Federal troops. Lee had 50,000 men left. Against these sick, weary Confederates, Grant had amassed a tremendous force of 280,000 well-equipped troops.

Longstreet, barely recovered from his wound, thought Grant might meet with Lee to discuss terms for peace. With President Davis's approval, a peace feeler letter was sent on March 2. But Grant could afford to be cool. Sheridan and Sherman, riding over the South, had helped lay

waste to the Confederacy. Mansions and crops were black ashes; slaughtered animals dotted the countryside.

When Lee received word of Sheridan's triumph, General John B. Gordon was called to Lee's quarters. From a long table covered with recent reports on all the Confederate armies' activities, Gordon began to read reports Lee handed him.

"The revelation was startling. Every report was bad . . ." Gordon realized.

When the analysis was completed, Lee took a seat facing Gordon at the table. Lee asked what Gordon thought the commanding general should do under "these conditions."

"General," Gordon replied, "it seems to me there are but three courses, and I name them in the order in which I think they should be tried."

First, Gordon said, ". . . make terms with the enemy; the best we can get."

Second, ". . . if that is not practical, the best thing to do is retreat. Abandon Richmond and Petersburg," march hard to link up with General Johnston in North Carolina and "strike Sherman before Grant can join him."

His final suggestion, Gordon said, was "fight and without delay."

Lee asked, "Is that your opinion?"

A little cautiously, as befits a lesser rank to the supreme commander, Gordon said it was. But he asked, wisely, how Lee saw the situation.

Lee replied, "Certainly, General. You have the right to ask my opinion. I agree with you fully."

But there were problems, Lee continued. As a soldier, he didn't have the right to use political action, which was required. Gordon did not know Davis had sent a peace feeler to Grant.

When the reply came, it was what might be expected from a foe who held all the power. Grant said, "I have no authority to accede to your proposition for a conference on the subject proposed. Such authority is vested in the President of the United States alone."

Lee went to see Davis. The president was firm. He would rather see the Confederacy go down fighting unless the Union would recognize independence for the Confederate States.

Lee might have expected such stubbornness from Davis who had held on to command of the army so long.

Lee came up with another plan. He could join Johnston, swing around and surprise Sherman, and then strike Grant. The surprise offensive-action, bold and daring as in the days of Jackson, might relieve the pressure on Richmond.

Since negotiation had failed to bring peace, Lee

went back to Petersburg prepared to fight. He had defeated Hooker, Burnside, McClellan, Meade and other top Union generals. Perhaps Grant might yet be added to the list.

A major offensive was launched March 25 at Fort Stedman. It was a bold plan such as Stonewall Jackson would have loved. It worked, it seemed, under General Gordon. His ragged Confederates surprised the Union defenders in a pre-dawn strike and spread out to grab off two near-by batteries.

But the Southern victory was short-lived. The great masses of Union reservists moved into the fight, overpowering the Confederates. Lee sat down the next day and explained his position to Davis:

"I fear now it will be impossible to prevent a junction between Grant and Sherman" and Lee didn't "deem it prudent" to keep his army in its present position until Grant got close. It was time to abandon Petersburg and Richmond, or go see Grant and get whatever peace terms Lee could.

The matter was decided the end of March when the Union triumphed at Five Points.

The desperateness of the Confederacy's situation was punctuated by a single bullet which a Union infantryman fired into the back of General A.P. Hill.

Four of Lee's top five generals had fallen since he planned the early 1863 campaigns. True, Longstreet had recovered and was able to join his troops, but Lee was a realist. The end of four years of terrible war was in sight as April dawned in 1865.

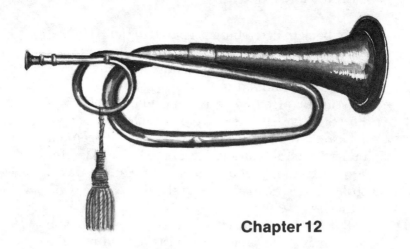

Appomattox Farewell

April, traditional time for beginning wars and launching new campaigns, saw Grant's massive 280,000 blue-coated soldiers ready to take the field. Lee's 65,000 (at the very most) weary troops reeled back under Federal attacks.

Lee sent word to Davis and the secretary of war urging, "all preparations be made for leaving Richmond." The cabinet fled that night by train, but it was too late.

Union troops were flooding over everything in Virginia and the rest of the Confederacy. The President and other officials became prisoners. Lee's son, Custis, along with other high-ranking Confederate officers, were taken by the massive hordes of onrushing Federals.

The news reached Lee of the events. He exclaimed, "Has the army been dissolved?"

As the first week of April ended, Grant sent three of his best officers to personally hand Lee a note. Lee read it: further resistance was hopeless. Surrender?

Lee handed the note to Longstreet. He answered: "Not yet."

But Lee was also a realist. He did what had to be done. What surrender terms did Grant propose?

What was left of the Army of Northern Virginia had been moving west, away from Richmond and Petersburg. The Union troops had taken the capital after it was abandoned. The siege at Petersburg had been successful for Grant.

Union soldiers were close behind the ragged Confederates. Rebel supplies were captured, and slowly escape routes were being shut by Grant's massive army. He was closing in on Lee.

On Saturday night, April 8, as Lee neared Appomattox Court House, Grant's latest letter came to him. Lee had been commander of the entire Confederate forces only two months and two days.

He replied to Grant, saying: "I did not intend to propose the surrender of the Army of Northern Virginia, but to ask the terms of your proposition."

Lee's words were brave, "I do not think the emergency has arisen to call for the surrender of this army, but as the restoration of peace should be the sole object of all, I desired to know whether these proposals would lead to that . . ."

Lee explained he could not meet with Grant "with a view to surrender the Army of Northern Virginia—but as far as your proposal may affect the Confederate States forces under my command, and tend to the restoration of peace, I shall be pleased to meet you at 10 a.m. tomorrow . . ."

As Lee had said earlier, "We have appealed to the God of battles, and He has decided against us."

Lee prepared for his meeting with Grant.

Other notes passed back and forth between the two men before final arrangements were made.

The meeting place was a two-story house with chimneys at either end and wide front steps leading up to the first floor's long porch. A similar porch with a white open woodwork balcony graced the second story. It was loaned by Wilmer McLean. He had moved from Manasses to escape the fighting. Now the war had caught up with him again. The McLean home was a part of a little-known village called Appomattox Court House. There was a tavern, a jail, a courthouse and a few homes.

But the war was not over, and fighting was still going on as Lee continued to exchange notes with Grant. Gordon's final effort to break out of the Federal lines had been made that very weekend. It was short-lived. The enormous Union forces swept in upon Gordon.

Soon word had come to Lee: "I have fought my troops to a frazzle," Gordon reported, "and I fear I can do nothing unless I am heavily supported by Longstreet."

But Longstreet could not come. Then Lee said the words which signaled the end of the conflict: "There is nothing left for me to do but go and see General Grant, and I would rather die a thousand deaths."

An officer asked, "What will history say of the surrender of this army in the field?"

Lee figured "they will say hard things of us. They will not understand how we were overwhelmed by numbers." Then Lee explained, "But that is not the question, Colonel. The question is: is it right to surrender this army? If it is right, then I will take all the responsibility."

Three generals came for a final proposal that they would urge their men to "take to the woods and bushes" where they would be as hard to catch as "rabbits and partridges."

In effect, this was a proposal for guerrilla warfare.

Lee wisely replied, "We must consider its effect on the country as a whole. If I took your advice, the men would be without rations and under no control of officers.

"They would be compelled to rob and steal in order to live. They would become mere bands of marauders, and the enemy's cavalry would pursue them and overrun many wide sections they may never have occasion to visit. We would bring on a state of affairs it would take the country years to recover from."

General E.P. Alexander, who had first proposed the idea, later wrote: "He [Lee] had answered my suggestion from a plane so far above it that I was ashamed of having made it."

Now all that was past. There was still talk of joining up with Johnston's troops, but it looked hopeless. Fitzhugh Lee's cavalry and Gordon's foot soldiers were engulfed by the overwhelming masses of Union troops west of Appomattox. Behind them, more blue-coated Federals could be seen moving up.

Lee had been up since 3 A.M. that Palm Sunday, April 9, 1865. Carefully, he dressed in his finest (and last) gray uniform. He pulled a silk sash about his middle, buckled on a ceremonial sword and mounted Traveller.

With Sergeant G.W. Tucker carrying a white flag and Colonel Charles Marshall riding along as an aide, Lee touched heels to his big gray horse.

Traveller picked his way through fog covering the field at Appomattox Court House. In the dawn's pale light, Lee saw an apple tree. The flowering tree was filled with the life of spring-time. Lee pulled Traveller up and rested under the tree. White blossoms occasionally floated to the ground while Lee waited for word from Grant. There was time to think.

Lee stayed under the apple tree, perhaps thinking of his oldest son, Custis, who had recently been taken prisoner. The war had cost Lee so heavily that a lesser man might have buckled under the load. But he had kept going, sustained by his unswerving belief in the God he served.

Finally, the general stirred as a courier from Grant advanced through the morning sun. "General Grant is coming, sir." Lee nodded. He touched his heels to the big gray horse.

In the distance firing was still flaring up in sporadic bursts as Lee moved toward the McLean house. Sergeant Tucker's flag of truce waved gently as he followed Lee's lead. Colonel Marshall rode ahead beside McLean to his home.

Some of Lee's men, not rolled up in the blanket of massive Federal forces sweeping everything before them, cheered their general as he passed. Then, slowly, as the full meaning of the white handkerchief on a stick in Tucker's hands struck them, the cheers died.

After some delays at Federal outposts, Lee and his small party moved up the hill toward Appomattox Court House. McLean led the way up the wide front steps of his home. Then Lee waited.

It was a long wait; well after one o'clock in the afternoon before Grant reined up outside. He had not slept. A sick headache had caused him to seek relief by soaking his feet in hot water and putting mustard plasters on the back of his neck and against his wrists. At 4 A.M., still suffering from the headache, he had taken to the road. It had taken a courier some time to find him.

He dismounted in front of McLean's steps.

Sheridan and other officers in blue tunics swung down from their saddles and trailed Grant into the room where Lee waited.

Grant looked as though he had spent a bad night. His face showed strain, and his clothes were soiled and dusty. Except for shoulder straps, his uniform gave no indication of rank.

At five feet, eight inches, he had to look up to Lee, who stood just under six feet. Grant was sixteen years younger than Lee. The two men varied in other ways. Grant's full beard was dark. He was a cigar-smoking, hard-drinking man— Lee's exact opposite.

Marshall, Lee's aide observed, "General Lee was standing at the end of the room opposite the door when General Grant walked in." Grant, his boots badly mud-spattered, pulled off his dark yellow gloves and tossed his stiff-brimmed hat on a table.

Grant walked across the room to Lee. "I met you once before, General Lee," the Union commander said, "in Mexico, when you came over from Scott's headquarters to visit Garland's Brigade."

Lee, immaculate in his uniform, shook hands as Grant continued. "I have always remembered your appearance, and I think I'd recognize you anywhere," Grant said in the clipped, sharp tones of his Northern accent.

The Confederate commander was honest. "Yes, I know I met you then, and I have often tried to recollect how you looked, but I have never been able to recall a single feature," Lee said softly, slurring his words together in Southern fashion.

There was an awkward silence as the roomful of blue-clad officers and the two gray-uniformed Lee aides watched. The generals spoke of Mexico and the weather.

Lee finally drew Grant's attention to the matter at hand. "I suppose, General Grant, that the object of our meeting is fully understood."

Grant replied that the surrender terms were about as stated in his letter of the day before: "that is, the officers and men surrendered to be paroled and disqualified from taking up arms again until properly exchanged, and all arms, ammunition and supplies to be delivered up as captured property."

Lee answered, "Those are about the conditions I expected would be proposed."

The two generals talked a little more. Then Grant called for Ely Parker, chief of the Six Nations, to bring writing materials.

The full-blooded Indian carried a small table to the Union general. Grant sat down, lit his pipe and puffed away as he thought a moment, then began to write.

When the rough draft was handed to Lee, he put on his glasses and read slowly and carefully. He suggested a couple of minor changes. A word was missing. Lee asked about it. Grant replied he had intended to put in the word "exchange" referring to prisoners.

"With your permission," Lee said, "I will mark where it should be inserted."

Grant nodded. "Certainly."

Lee had no pencil. A Union colonel handed his over. Lee thanked him, made the insertion and continued reading.

Lee touched his spectacles thoughtfully. The next condition proposed by Grant directly affected the dress sword Lee had worn to the meeting. The pact read, "This will not embrace the side arms of the officers, or their private horses or baggage."

Grant had deliberately written the surrender

terms so that Lee would not have to suffer the embarrassment of having to hand over his sword. It was improper, under Grant's own terms, for Grant to ask for Lee's sword.

Lee continued reading the surrender document: ". . . each officer and man will be allowed to return to their homes not to be disturbed by United States authorities so long as they observe their paroles and the laws in force where they may reside. Very respectfully, U.S. Grant, Lt. Gl."

Lee looked up from the table toward Grant. "This will have a very happy effect on my army."

Grant said that unless Lee had other suggestions on the agreement, "I will have a copy of the letter made in ink and sign it."

For a moment, Lee hesitated. "There is one thing I would like to mention," he said. "The cavalrymen and artillerymen in our army own their own horses. Our organization differs from yours. I would like to understand whether these men will be permitted to retain their horses?"

Grant pointed out that "the terms as written do not allow this."

Thoughtfully, Lee read the second page. "No, I see the terms do not allow it. That's clear."

Grant saw in Lee's face the desire to have this change made. Grant was the victor. He could afford to be generous. But he also had an edge to keep.

"I will arrange it this way," he said. "I will not change the terms as they are written, but I will instruct the officers to let all the men who claim to own a horse or mule take the animals home with them to work their little farms."

Lee was pleased. "This will have the best possible effect upon the men. It will be very gratifying and will do much toward reconciliating our people."

Small talk was made as the Indian drew up the ink copy. Grant called up his officers and introduced them. Some offered their right hands. Lee shook those. He bowed to the men who did not offer to shake hands. Then Lee turned back to Grant.

"I have a thousand or more of your men as prisoners," Lee said. "I shall be glad to send them into your lines as soon as it can be arranged, for I have no provisions for them."

Perhaps thinking that might sound selfish, Lee added, "I have, indeed, nothing for my own men. They have been living for the last few days principally upon parched corn, and are badly in need of both rations and forage." He said he had telegraphed Lynchburg for supplies which should supply his men when the trainloads arrived.

The Union officers glanced at Sheridan. He had seized those same Confederate supplies the night before. Lee had not yet been informed. Grant didn't see any need to embarrass Lee by mentioning the facts. "I will take steps at once to have your army supplied with rations, but I am sorry we have no forage for animals." He asked how many men Lee had.

"Indeed, I am not able to say." Lee explained that losses had been heavy and all his papers had been destroyed to keep them from falling into Federal hands. "I have no means of ascertaining our present strength," he concluded.

The Union commander asked, "Suppose I send over twenty-five thousand rations? Do you think that will be a sufficient supply?"

Lee nodded. "I think it will be ample. And it will be a great relief, I assure you."

The surrender papers were ready. Lee ordered Marshall to copy them. Then Lee picked up the

pen. Addressed to Grant from Lee, the document
was simple:

> *I have received your letter of this date con-*
> *taining the terms of surrender of the Army of*
> *Northern Virginia as proposed by you. As*
> *they are substantially the same as those ex-*
> *pressed in your letter of the 8th instant, they*
> *are accepted. I proceed to designate the*
> *proper officers to carry the stipulations into*
> *effect. Very respectfully, your obedient*
> *servant.*

Lee signed it, then arose and shook hands with
Grant. Lee bowed to the others and walked down
the hall onto the long porch. Federal officers there
snapped to attention. They saluted smartly. Lee
put on his hat and returned the salute, then pulled
on his gloves.

For a moment, the gray-bearded man who had
just surrendered his army stood looking across the
valley. His troops, not yet aware the war was over,
lay on a hillside where their observers surely had
seen the famous gray Traveller standing with
Union horses.

Lee brought his gloved hands together in
several sharp smacks. "Orderly!" His voice was
deep in his throat and a little unsteady. "Orderly!"

Sergeant Tucker brought Traveller into sight.
Lee stuck his foot into the stirrup and swung into
the saddle. He settled into the leather with a sigh
clearly heard by the onlookers.

Grant walked onto the porch and down the
steps. Before he reached the gate, he stopped
abruptly and swept his hat from his head before
Lee. The other Union officers did the same.

Nobody spoke. Lee, keeping the silence, raised
his hat, and turned Traveller out of the McLean
yard.

As he rode down the lane, his soldiers started to cheer him. But there was something about Lee's appearance and the things they had seen which caused their cheers to slide uncertainly back into their throats.

They swept toward him. Someone asked the question they were not ready to believe: "General, are we surrendered?"

For a moment, it appeared Lee tried to ignore the question. He urged Traveller forward, but the hungry, sick and valiant men swarmed toward Lee.

"In an instant, they were about him; bareheaded, with tear-wet faces; thronging him, kissing his hand, his boots, his saddle—weeping, cheering him amid their tears, shouting his name to the very skies," a soldier related.

Lee reined in the big gray horse. Lee bared his gray head. "Men," he said, "we have fought through the war together. I have done my best for you. My heart is too full to say more."

Tears flowed down his bearded cheeks as he moved toward a tree down the road. He dismounted and began to pace, apparently feeling for the first time the impact of what he had done. His officers left him alone in the late afternoon of that Sunday in April 1865.

After four terrible years, the Civil War was over.

Robert E. Lee, Christian general and gentleman, wrote his last order to the army he had led so long and well. "After four years of arduous service, marked by unsurpassed courage and fortitude, the Army of Northern Virginia has been compelled to yield to overwhelming numbers and resources," he began.

He paid tribute to the "survivors of so many hard-fought battles" and said he had determined "to avoid the useless sacrifice of those whose past services have endeared them to their countrymen."

He explained that men could return to their homes until exchanged. They were really prisoners of war, paroled to their homes.

"I earnestly pray that a merciful God will extend to you His blessing and protection," Lee added, then concluded, "I bid you an affectionate farewell."

In a few days, Lee took off the sword he had sworn to never raise again except in defense of his native state. After forty years in uniform, Lee was again a private citizen.

Chapter 13

€ollege President

Robert E. Lee, private citizen, rode Traveller into the fire-blackened ruins of Richmond on Saturday, April 15. There was rubble everywhere. Brick shells stood like ghostly tombstones to the memory of the Confederate capital.

But there were worse ghosts ahead. The previous evening, President Abraham Lincoln had been shot at Ford's Theater in Washington. He had clung to life during the night. The next morning the president died. The dramatic and unexpected turn of events had far-reaching results over the South.

Lincoln had been firm in pressing for preservation of the Union as one nation. He had indicated he was willing to "let 'em up easy," a reference to forgiveness of the Confederates. He had urged the country to bind up its wounds and go on as one nation.

But the assassin's bullet smashed Lincoln's life and his plan. Bitterness against the South flowed

like Lincoln's own blood. General Lee became the
target of vicious Northern newspaper attacks.

The morning after Lincoln died, Lee took his
family to St. Paul's Church in Richmond. It was
natural for him, for, in war or peace, in victory
or defeat, Lee trusted in the sacred steadfastness
of His Savior.

He had no home. He had lost all except some
investments. Word had come in early 1864 that
Arlington was forever lost as a result of Union
taxation. When one of Lee's cousins tried to pay
the $28,800 taxes due, his offer was refused. The
Union insisted the owner appear in person and
pay the back taxes. Since that had been impossible
for Lee, Lee lost his wife's ancestral home. The
home, however, had begun a new phase.

In May, a Confederate soldier had been buried
on the grounds. On June 15, 210 acres near
Arlington House were made a national military
cemetery. In time, Arlington National Cemetery
became the final resting place of the nation's
Unknown Soldier and President John Kennedy,
among others.

Lee had only some surviving family members,
his poor health, and his untarnished faith left to
him. His faith had remained firm during the war,
and it remained steady in the peace-with-trouble
which raged around him.

Newspapers called him a traitor and urged a
treason trial. In June 1865 Lee was indicted with
others on treason charges. The United States
Grand Jury in Norfolk, Virginia, made the formal
charges.

"How can they try Marse Lee?" questioned an
indignant former soldier.

"It is well to remember that if George
Washington had lost the American Revolutionary

War, he would have faced similar charges from England," assured a calm friend.

"Well, they'll clear him," stormed the soldier. "They'd better, I tell you."

Lee remained calm in the midst of the postwar hysteria—as calm as when he had sat on Traveller's broad back in the midst of battle.

When someone criticized the North in a Richmond gathering, Lee waited until afterward. He quietly approached the outspoken critic.

"I have fought against the people of the North," he explained, "because I believed that they were seeking to wrest from the South dearest rights. But I have never cherished toward them bitter or vindictive feelings, and have never seen the day when I did not pray for them."

The war had punished him severely. He was fifty-eight years old, but some said he looked older. But he took up what was left of his life and went on, doing what he thought was right, in peace.

That summer, Lee moved his family from Richmond to a small house near Cartersville. There was no St. Paul's Episcopal Church in the village as in Richmond. But, as a neighbor said, "During the summer, he was a regular attendant at the various churches in our neighborhood, whenever there was service."

Lee's life took on a positive new direction on Friday, August 4. Just four months after the surrender, a somewhat hesitant man wearing a borrowed suit suggested Lee would make a good college president. Lee had been offered other positions, but this one from Washington College in Lexington, Virginia, prompted Lee to seek counsel of his friend, Bishop Joseph P. Wilmer.

"I congratulated him that his heart was inclined

to this great cause," the bishop said in urging Lee
to accept the $1,500-a-year position, "and that he
was spared to give the world this education."

The Washington College buildings were run-
down and in disrepair from the war. But that
didn't bother Lee. "I accepted the presidency of
this college," he said, "in the hope that I might be
of some service to the country, and the rising
generation, and not from any preference of my
own." His personal preference was for "a more
quiet life," and he would "have preferred a small
farm where I could earn my daily bread."

He moved his family to the president's home
on campus.

Enrollment at the college tripled within a year.
It kept growing over the years as Lee began to
build young men for citizenship in the shattered
part of what was once again the United States of
America. Among his new duties was sharing his
own faith with the students at Washington
College.

"I dread the thought of any student going away
from the college without becoming a sincere
Christian," Lee declared.

Someone asked him why he was so thoughtful
coming out of college chapel one morning. Lee
replied, "I was thinking of my responsibility to
Almighty God for these hundreds of young men."

The radical Northern press continued to attack
Lee with vicious words. He kept his peace.

Lee was called to Washington. He was
examined by a congressional committee and
released after saying very little. He didn't do much
visiting on the way home, passing by the homes of
friends.

"I am now considered such a monster that I
hesitate to darken with my shadows the doors of
those I love best, lest I should bring upon them

misfortune," he explained. The "Old Rebel," as
he sometimes referred to himself, was not being
bitter. He was simply stating the facts.

Lee was not brought to trial on treason charges,
but the possible trial hung on so long that Lee
decided to take some action. Many a loud voice
still demanded Lee be hanged. But Lee saw a
proper legal move to make.

A letter was sent to Grant, saying Lee was ready
to be tried if the matter was to come to that. But if
he was not to be arraigned, Lee was applying for a
pardon.

It was a good approach. Other Southerners took
the same tact. Grant's weight helped Lee avoid
trial, but the pardon was not granted. The issue
dragged on, with some dramatic side effects.

Many old soldiers came to see Lee after the war.
Some urged him to flee into the mountains where
he could not be tried for treason.

"You would not have your general run away and
hide," he chided them. "He must stay here and
meet his fate."

Thousands of letters poured in. The people
loved him. Patiently, Lee answered as best he
could, encouraging them to stand firm in their
faith and to help heal the wounds of war.

As Lee's mind turned more and more to
education of the students at Washington College,
great military heads journeyed from Europe to the
United States to study, firsthand, the fantastic
tactics he had used against better equipped and
more numerous forces. They praised Lee as the
greatest military genius of the century.

A military man said, "Lee's campaigns of 1862
are . . . supreme in conception, and have not
been surpassed, as examples of strategy . . . by
any other commander in history."

Lee paid little attention. He had done his duty

as he saw it, in war and peace; to Virginia and to God. Lee was true to both his state and his God, and Lee was content to trust in Divine Providence to do what was right.

Lee's health continued to bother him in those early postwar years. He was subjected to constant crowds of cheering, adoring people whenever he went out in public. This taxed his waning strength, but he would not stay cooped up away from people.

Mary, his wife, was worried. "He looks fatter," she wrote their daughter, Mildred, "but I do not like his complexion, and he seems stiff."

Some Southerners decried the new president of

the country. It was Ulysses S. Grant—the man Lee had known well in war. Lee held no ill feelings and said little.

On Wednesday, September 28, 1870, Lee left his office at the college at the end of a routine day. He went home briefly, then walked through the autumn rain to a vestry meeting at the church.

He was one of the laymen who conducted the church's business. Lee sat through the meeting in the chilly room. There was no heat, and Lee wore only his old military cape and a hat. Still, some churchmen noticed that Lee's face seemed somewhat flushed, even in the cold room.

As chairman, Lee wound up the evening's

business about seven o'clock. There was a final
item: about $55 was still needed to meet the
rector's salary.

Lee said softly, "I will give that sum."

He walked out into the night and across to the
house the college provided for him. He never
referred to it as "my house," but always as "the
president's home." How unlike lost Arlington
House it was.

He came in out of the hard, cold rain, hung up
his hat and cape and came to the table—late. That
was not like Lee. When his children were little and
Mary was late for church or other places Lee had
sometimes gone ahead without her so he would
not be tardy.

But that was a long time ago, Mary reflected as
he came to the table. She was confined to her
rolling chair, but she smilingly teased her husband
about being late that September night. "You have
kept us waiting a long time. Where have you
been?"

Lee did not answer. He stood in his regular
place in front of his chair, ready to say the blessing.
It was a familiar routine in the Lee home. But that
rainy night, Lee could not speak.

Suddenly, he fell back in his chair.

There was nothing else unusual about Lee's
manner in that moment. He was as calm as though
he had been in the midst of shot and shell, astride
Traveller, instead of stricken speechless and
collapsed in the last chair in which he would ever
sit.

His wife tried to be calm. "You look very tired.
Let me pour you a cup of tea."

Still, Lee did not speak. Agnes, his third
daughter, studied him anxiously. Mary called for
Custis, the Lee's oldest son. He called for the
doctors.

They put Lee to bed in front of a living room window where he had liked to sit and look out. Doctors came, but there was no medicine for this illness. Now, in the bed they had brought in for him, Lee's life ebbed slowly away.

A storm beat across the countryside in the next several days. The streams rose and the waters rushed in floods, just as they had during the war. The waters gobbled up homes and trees as September slid into October.

For eight days the rains fell in miserable torrents upon the Lee's rented home. Bridges and communications were washed away. In the deluge rivers spread across fields into streets. The town's entire supply of caskets was even swept away from the funeral parlor.

Lee did not know about the prolonged storm. His mind had gone free, past the ramparts of rain and flood. He again roamed the battlefields where duty called. Once he said aloud, "Tell Hill he *must* come up."

About nine o'clock in the morning of October 12, Mildred ran for the doctor. He came, looked at Lee, then turned slowly away. The doctor kept his head bowed.

Others gathered around the dying figure on the bed. That bright October morning they heard the village clock strike the half-hour. Lee's voice suddenly filled the room. It was clear and strong, as it had been in the fields of battle.

"Strike the tent!"

Lee had given his last order to move on. He departed to a place of eternal peace with his Savior.

The word of Lee's death spread around the nation and the world. The chapel bell began to toll the sad news. Other church bells echoed it.

Schools closed. Businesses stopped. Buildings were draped in black.

Even his enemies were at peace with him now. The newspapers which had screamed for his hanging had lost their favorite whipping boy.

The *New York Tribune*, whose unfavorable opinions of Lee had caught his attention in life, sent a reporter to cover Lee's funeral. The reporter found the "town overwhelmed with grief." The only topic of conversation in Lexington was the death of General Lee. This was true "at the hotels, by the hearthstone, in the schools, on the streets . . . All classes of the community seem to be affected; even the colored people, who walk along in silence with sorrowful countenance and mourn the loss of 'Good ol' Marse Robert.' "

There were no caskets available until schoolboys came upon an unused coffin which had been swept away by the floods. This was recovered and taken into Lexington. There it was found the five-foot, eleven-inch general was slightly too long for the casket. They removed his shoes, and Lee was buried in his stocking feet.

Many important state officials were present, along with students and old soldiers, as Lee's body was lowered into the grave prepared in the chapel basement.

In time, the name of the college was changed. No longer was it simply honoring the first president, Washington. The college became Washington and Lee to commemorate both famous Virginians.

And so, after sixty-three years, all that was mortal of Robert E. Lee was buried in Virginia, the state which he loved and defended with all that was in him.

In defeat, Lee became one of the most

respected men on the face of the earth. As the years passed, he was more and more honored. His example continues to shine through the first century of his passing with an undimmed luster that grows ever brighter.

Without doubt, he was one of the most remarkable men this nation ever produced. He set an example for all people of all ages to follow. And he set the example so high no one can easily reach it.

He finished high and well in the halls of fame, yet history itself has exalted him beyond his lifetime. This continuing recognition of Robert E. Lee caused the Congress of the United States, with signature of the president, to grant Lee a pardon one hundred five years after his death. In 1975, Lee's citizenship was restored as a further demonstration of the honor men still hold for him.

Robert E. Lee, Christian general and gentleman, had discovered the secret of living the life made possible in Christ.

BIBLIOGRAPHY

Alexander, E. P. *Military Memoirs of a Confederate*. Scribners.

Carter, Hodding. *R. E. Lee and the Road of Honor*. Random House.

Davis, Burke. *Gray Fox, Robert E. Lee and the Civil War*. New York: Rinehart & Company, Inc., 1956.

Dowdey, Clifford. *Lee*. Boston: Little Brown & Co.

Fishwick, Marshall W. *Lee After the War, the Greatest Period in the Life of a Great American*. Dodd, Mead & Co., 1963.

Freeman, Douglas Southall. *R. E. Lee, a Biography*. 4 vols. New York: Charles Scribner's Sons.

Gerson, Noel B. *Light-Horse Harry, a Biography of Washington's Great Cavalryman, General Henry Lee*. Doubleday.

Gordon, John B. *Reminiscenses of the Civil War*. Scribners.

Harwell, Richard. *Lee, an Abridgement of Vol. 4, Freeman*. Scribners.

Johnstone, William J. *Robert E. Lee - The Christian*. Abington Press, 1933.

Lee, Robert E. *Recollections and Letters of General Lee*. Doubleday, 1924.

Meredith, Roy. *The Face of Robert E. Lee in Life and Legend*. New York: Charles Scribner's Sons, 1947.

Miers, Earl Schenck. *Robert E. Lee, a Great Life in Brief*. Alfred A. Knopf.

Sanborn, Margaret. *Robert E. Lee, a Portrait, 1807-1861*. J. B. Lippincott, 1966.

Taylor, Walter H. *Four Years with General Lee*. New York: D. Appleton Co., 1877.

Van Doren Stern, Philip. *Robert E. Lee The Man and The Soldier (a pictorial biography)*. New York: Bonanza Books, 1963.

INDEX

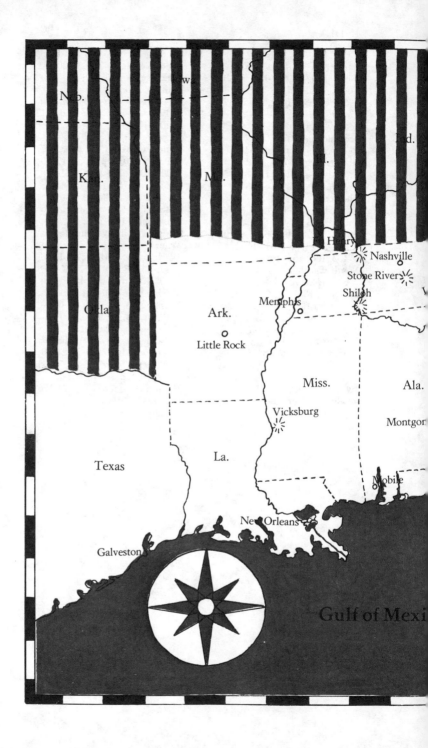

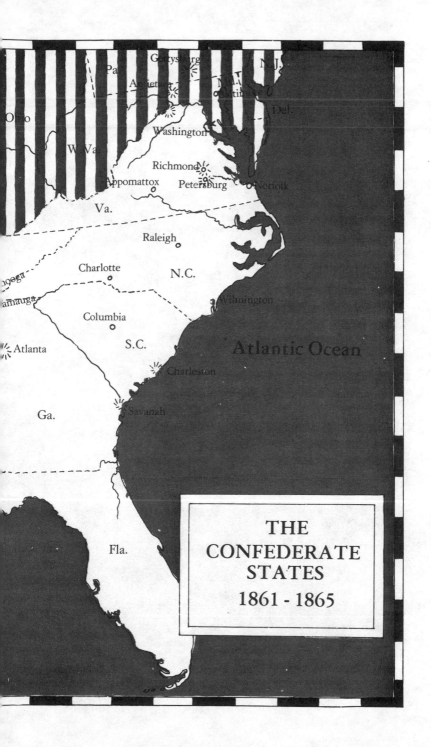

Ohio

Gettysburg

Pa.

N.J.

Antietam

Md.

Baltimore

W.Va.

Del.

Washington

Richmond

Appomattox

Petersburg

Norfolk

Va.

Raleigh

Charlotte

N.C.

anooga

amauga

Wilmington

Columbia

Atlanta

S.C.

Charleston

Ga.

Savanah

Atlantic Ocean

Fla.

**THE
CONFEDERATE
STATES
1861 - 1865**

SOWERS SERIES